(continued from front flap)

the American labor movement, first as research director for the Hosiery Workers Union, then as organizer for the Philadelphia Committee for Industrial Organization, finally as Washington representative of the Textile Workers Union.

During his long career, John Edelman was deeply involved in many basic social and political issues. Public housing was of particular interest to him, and he was instrumental in getting federal money for the first real workers' housing project in the United States—the Carl Mackley Houses in Philadelphia. In the split among unions over organizing by craft or by industry, he took the side of industry-wide organizing. He also played a significant role in the passage of legislation for the St. Lawrence Seaway and redevelopment of depressed areas. Other movements that received his hard-working attention were consumer protection, workers' education, battles against yellow-dog contracts, and the use of injunctions against unions.

Here is no dry recitation of legislative battles fought and won, but a sparkling narrative of events and people. Here are capsule portraits of the leaders of labor—John L. Lewis, Philip Murray, George Meany—and the political leaders in Washington in the thirties, forties, fifties, and sixties. Here are many of the great issues that have faced the labor movement during the past five decades as they were witnessed and lived by a man of urbanity and passion.

JOSEPH CARTER is the au
books, including *1918: Year
of Change.*

John W. Edelman

This is a biography, true, but also a pretty good novel as the story unfolds, and a superb treatise on sociology. No student of recent American history, and especially of the labor movement, can afford to neglect it. John Edelman was right in the middle of the profound shift from craft unions to industrial unions in the 1930s, and right in the middle of the profound changes in the status of American workers generated by the New Deal. He was a friend and co-worker of Eleanor Roosevelt, Walter Reuther, John Kennedy, Philip Murray, Paul Douglas, and many others. He was a leader in promoting workers' education, public housing, minimum wages, social security. He even helped to wangle the St. Lawrence Seaway

The novel reaches a climax when Congress finally passes th Medicare bill. Without the devoted work of John Edelman many believe that this great reform might have been pos poned for years. His last episode tells of the historic flight President Johnson and a distinguished company in two a force jets to Independence, Missouri. There, in the presen of an ailing Mr. Truman, Medicare was duly signed into la to change the lives of millions of Americans.

—STUART CHASE, author of *The Most Probable Wo*

LABOR LOBBYIST

Other Books by Joseph Carter

History of the 14th Armored Division
Death and Four Lovers
1918: Year of Crisis, Year of Change
Raging Bull (*with Jake LaMotta*)
Nothing to Kick About (*with Peter Gogolak*)

LABOR LOBBYIST

The Autobiography of

John W. Edelman

edited by Joseph Carter

The Bobbs-Merrill Company, Inc.
INDIANAPOLIS · NEW YORK

Published by the Bobbs-Merrill Company, Inc.
Indianapolis New York

ISBN 0-672-51677-2
Library of Congress catalog card number 73-1729
Designed by Paula Wiener
Manufactured in the United States of America
First printing

For

KATE VAN EATON EDELMAN

A Rebel in Her Own Right

LABOR LOBBYIST

Chapter One

THE MOST DRAMATIC moment of my young life occurred on February 2, 1901, when I was seven and one-half years old, at Waterloo Station in London.

Drenched in martial music and glittering with flags, the interior of the station, a vast, cavernous building, was ablaze with light. Across the way, a company of bearded, turbaned Sikhs stood at attention, their drawn sabers reflecting quivers of steel. A brilliantly uniformed detachment of a Guards regiment went stamping by, left arms swinging stiffly, right arms gripping their rifles.

I was spellbound.

What had happened?

Victoria, queen of Great Britain and empress of India, had died.

Her death had occurred at Osborne House, the royal residence on the Isle of Wight, and there she had been laid in state in an extraordinary ceremony in which no undertakers were allowed to take part. She had been displayed in death clad all in white—a request she had made of Lord Tennyson

—lying beneath a huge Union Jack suspended from the ceiling. Her grandson, Kaiser Wilhelm II, he of the withered left arm, had taken the flag back to Germany as a souvenir. The royal yacht *Alberta* had brought her body back to England, from where it was being taken by train for burial at Windsor Castle.

I was present at this scene of pomp and grandeur because my father had died six months earlier in New York City; my mother's brother, Senia Krimont, a Black Sea grain trader who lived in London, had asked our family to come and live with him until we could get settled.

We had just arrived at Waterloo Station, off the boat train from Southampton: my mother, Rachelle Krimont Edelman; my five-and-one-half-year-old sister, Sonia; an old family friend named Harry Kelly; and I.

Kelly was the sort of man my family would have for a friend. By most people's standards he was, to put it gently, an eccentric; he was a rarity—a home-grown American anarchist. Born on a farm in Missouri, raised in total poverty, he had entered the noble fraternity of tramp printers and had finally risen to his present station in life: London-based representative of an American printing-equipment manufacturer called American Typefounders. He made his sales calls wearing a gray top hat and morning coat—a fine figure of a man—and was the mate of my aunt, Mary Krimont, who had given him a daughter, Elsie.

I say "mate" rather than husband because my Aunt Mary, like a surprisingly large number of other "advanced" young ladies of the day, refused to take part in a ceremony requiring her to "love, honor, and obey" a man.

Kelly had met my Aunt Mary at my parents' home. He and my parents, drawn together first by their mutual devotion to anarchism, had become great friends in New York. (I use "anarchism" in its classic sense: a group of people living communally without formally constituted authority.) So when Senia Krimont had invited the Edelman family to stay with him, Kelly had arranged a business trip to America so that he could escort us to London.

My father, John H. Edelmann, was well known in the field of American architecture. (My generation dropped the second "n" in the name.) He was of German extraction, of a family whose name was originally Edelmann von Lilienthal in the records of Lower Saxony. The "von Lilienthal" was dropped when my father's parents fled the revolution of 1848 and settled in Cleveland, Ohio, where he was born in 1852.

Ironically, for a man who was to become so devoted an anarchist, my father's parents fled the German revolution not because they thought it would fail but because they, members of the minor nobility, feared it would succeed.

By 1873, my father had become foreman of the architectural offices of William Le Baron Jenney in Chicago, where one of the apprentices was a man later to become world famous—Louis Sullivan. It was not unusual in those days for a youth to apprentice himself in an architect's office at the age of sixteen, as my father had done, so it was not remarkable that he was foreman at twenty-one. The Jenney firm is famous for having built the world's first skyscraper, the Home Insurance Building in Chicago. Though it was only twelve stories high, its fame rests on its having been the first building in which a framework of steel supported the weight of the floors and the walls—the principle of the skyscraper.

Of my father, Louis Sullivan once wrote: "You can make up your mind that my reputation as an architect will always be inferior to his."

That turned out to be a mistaken prophecy. What made Sullivan famous, apart from his genius, was that he thought, dreamed, and lived nothing but architecture; architecture was his whole life. My father, on the other hand, was involved in so many projects that I don't see how he designed as much as he did. A fair baritone and a devotee of Wagnerian concerts, he was also an excellent amateur oarsman; he loved horses and both bred and raced them; and he was a sculptor, a painter, an anarchist, and a Single Taxer. When he left the Jenney firm in Chicago and moved to New York, for example, it was not to further his architectural career but to help direct Henry George's campaign for mayor in 1886.

Henry George, following the publication of his book *Progress and Poverty,* in which he made his case for the Single Tax, had become a towering figure in the late nineteenth century. His reputation had led to his nomination for mayor, a race that he lost by only 22,000 votes. It was at a Single Tax rally for Henry George that my mother and father met.

I have no idea what influenced my father to become an anarchist and in general a political left-winger. The last surviving member of his generation, he died when I was still far too young to understand the adult world. I know exactly, however, why my mother moved in those circles; she came of a background of Russian Jewish intellectual rebels. My maternal grandfather was Jacob Krimont, chief forester for Czar Alexander II in the province of the Ukraine. (His duties also included supervising the vast grain farms of the Ukraine.) The chief forester for an area of approximately 250,000 square miles—almost the size of Texas—does not spend much time in the woods. Krimont lived in Odessa and had a large suite of offices and a staff in a government office building still standing today at the top of "The 200 Steps," a wide stone stairway that leads down to the Black Sea. Important enough to be one of the few Jews in Russia allowed to own private real estate, he ran a ménage that included a library, two living rooms, eight bedrooms for the family and six for the servants, plus a carriage house for six horses with an apartment above for the coachman and his wife.

There existed a fierce intellectual tradition in the family. Both parents were well educated and gifted conversationalists, both had a wide range of interests, and both were intellectual anarchists. Krimont had sent his son Senia and a daughter Sophie (there were two sons and seven daughters in my mother's generation of the Krimont family) to the University of St. Petersburg, one of the first universities in the world to admit women as students. Both children had been expelled because of their anarchist views. The Krimont family was well enough known so that when on one occasion Tolstoi visited Odessa, he was entertained at the Krimont household. My mother, about five years old at the time, remembered Tolstoi, big and bearded, lifting her up onto his lap.

"His beard tickled," she told me.

Alexander II was the great social reformer among the czars of Russia, but after his assassination, which occurred on the very day that he signed a ukase that would have virtually transformed Russia into a constitutional monarchy, his son Alexander III turned out to be a very different cup of tea. He abolished the ukase and instituted a program of persecution of both students and intellectuals, as well as a series of pogroms against the Jews.

Regardless of their status, it was impossible that the Krimonts of Odessa would not be eventual victims. Odessa was the scene of almost nightly anti-Semitic riots; mobs stormed through the streets at will seeking out Jews. My mother remembered the servants—Russian Orthodox down to the last kitchen maid—hanging crosses in the windows and on the doors to protect the house.

Jacob Krimont decided to flee Russia. He sold all the possessions he could and moved his family to Bucharest, only a way station, of course, for the Krimonts dreamed, like all oppressed Europeans, of moving to America. Senia, the elder son, was sent ahead, traveling steerage with a group of Rumanian Jews headed for New York. There Senia joined a group of about a dozen other young Jewish men and women, all refugees, whose aim was to found an anarchist colony somewhere in the United States. They called themselves "Am Olam," meaning "The Eternal People."

The site they chose for the colony was in the state of Oregon, near a small town called Glendale. The reason for this choice was Henry Villard. Villard, who had emigrated from Germany to America in 1853, had already become renowned in his adopted country as a newspaperman (publisher of the *New York Evening Post*) and industrialist (a founder of the General Electric Company and board chairman of the Northern Pacific Railway). On one of his trips to Oregon in connection with financial arrangements for his eventual takeover of the Northern Pacific, Villard, very active in Jewish affairs in

New York—he was one of the original sponsors of "Am Olam"—had fallen in love with the unspoiled Oregon wilderness. He talked the young colonists into relocating there.

They worked their way across the country, mostly by farm labor, and, once there, Senia wrote to his family of the joys of Oregon. Within a few months they followed him—by boat to Panama, across Panama by train, and up the West Coast of America by boat to Portland, Oregon. With their arrival, and that of a few others from New York, the colony—called "New Odessa"—was officially formed.

The land chosen for the colony was comprised of some 750 acres, hilly and heavily timbered, 150 acres of which were under cultivation. In addition to the two small farmhouses already on the land, the colonists built a large two-story frame community center, the upper floor a dormitory for single men at one end, single women at the other. The beds were simple, handmade wooden cots set in rows, and in the center of the main hall stood a large homemade wooden table for reading and writing. There was also a small library. The farmhouses were partitioned off for the use of the families.

In the colony's first two years, an additional fifty acres of land were cultivated, the main crops being wheat, oats, beans, and peas to be sold, and a variety of vegetables for home consumption. The colonists lived on what they grew, supplemented by fish they caught in the rivers and rabbits and an occasional deer they shot in the woods. According to their records, the daily food budget for items they had to buy—salt, for example—was between five and eight cents per person.

Obviously, they still needed money. Besides having to buy items they couldn't make or raise themselves—nails, shoes, clothes, coffee, shotgun shells, to name a few—they had a mortgage to pay off.

The land had cost forty-eight hundred dollars, of which the first two thousand had been put up by the supporters of "Am Olam" in New York. A number of the colonists had found jobs in neighboring Glendale—some were skilled machinists and could contribute more to the colony by working outside it—but the really big revenue-producing item was logging, which provided railroad ties and fuel for the woodburning locomotives of the Oregon & California Railroad, then being built south from Portland to San Francisco. In the first two years of its existence, the colony received payments totaling almost eight thousand dollars from the railroad.

In this Garden of Eden, the serpent was to turn out to be a colonist named Frey. A Russian nobleman, an officer in the armies of Alexander II, a former professor of mathematics in the Russian Military Academy at St. Petersburg, Frey was a disciple of the French philosopher August Comte, who believed that a perfect society could be achieved by explaining phenomena through observation, hypothesis, and experiment. (He coined the word sociology to cover the range of his beliefs.) Also a vegetarian, Frey not only abstained from eating meat himself but refused to sit at the same table with anyone who did.

Frey—apparently a fascinating and persuasive talker—converted a number of colonists to his beliefs; a split developed in the colony that did not end even after he had left, taking fifteen of the colonists with him: quite a blow since to begin with there had been a total of only about thirty-five.

The dissension that continued after Frey's departure rose over whether the commune was a viable social concept. The arguments grew more bitter every day, and finally the end came. The assets of the colony were divided as equitably as possible, and most of the colonists, the Krimonts among them, returned to New York.

Three changes had taken place in the Krimont family in the few short years at New Odessa. The father, Jacob, had died only a few months after the birth of his ninth child and second son, Arnold, in 1883, and the oldest girl, Sophie, had married a fellow colonist, Alexander Kislick.

Back in New York, money was short and family skills were few. For a time all the children old enough worked in laundries; then the family moved to Fall River, Massachusetts, having learned that the weaving mills there were hiring workers. After a few months at the trades of weaving and spinning, the family decided to move back to New York. There the different members of the family got a variety of jobs, studied evenings at Cooper Union, and naturally, because of their upbringing, began to move in the radical, cosmopolitan circles of the day.

In a remarkably short span of time, they began to go their separate ways. Clare, one of my six aunts, married a lanky young fellow from Ulster named John S. Steele, later a renowned newspaperman for the *Chicago Tribune*. (I mention him because of the role he was to play later in my life.) My grandmother died early in 1889. Senia returned to Europe to begin work as a Black Sea grain trader, his headquarters in London. And my mother, Rachelle, then twenty years old, met John H. Edelmann at a Single Tax rally for Henry George.

They were married within a matter of months, taking the youngest Krimont child, Arnold, to live with them in a house that Edelmann had built in Forest Hill, New Jersey, then a rustic, tree-grown village but now a part of the urban sprawl of Newark.

There I was born on June 27, 1893, and my sister Sonia followed a little over two years later. Just a few years after that, my father died in a fall from the construction scaffolding of a nearly completed Fifth Avenue mansion for which he was the supervising architect.

Senia Krimont then extended his invitation for the entire family to join him in London; thus we had all arrived at Waterloo Station that morning in February 1901.

Chapter Two

THE LONDON world into which the Edelman family moved was a world of contrasts. It was a world of the glory of royalty, the glamour of the race meets at Epsom Downs, the splendor of ceremony. At the same time it was a world of squalid slums in which whole families lived in a single room, from grandparent to grandchild, sleeping, eating, defecating, copulating, being born and dying, all within sound, if not sight, of one another. A world in which a skilled cigar maker earned thirteen cents an hour, worked seventeen hours a day, seven days a week, and started his children helping him full time when they were ten. A world of despair, from which only death brought release. Yet on the whole, it was, to my mind, a world at peace, a world of gaslight and hansom cabs, quieter and more leisurely by far than the world of today. Most important of all for me, it was a world of intellectual ferment.

The theory that society as a whole owes responsibility to the poor had already been born. Karl Marx had written *Das Kapital;* Henry Mayhew, his monumental *London Labour and the London Poor;* Charles Dickens, *Oliver Twist;* Sidney and Beatrice Webb, *Industrial Democracy.*

The theory of the role of the state in the lives of the poor marked, I think, a major change in the political thinking of the nineteenth century. Up to that point, all of society, including the poor themselves, regarded poverty as a condition in which one was born and lived one's life—unless the individual were one of the fortunate few gifted with brains, ingenuity, nerve, or luck. The Biblical observation that "the poor ye have always with you" was accepted literally. Then in the nineteenth century came the concept that the state had a duty to the poor; they were not there simply to be exploited for the profit of the factory owner, the landlord, or the farm proprietor. This concept, and its acceptance, became the great force of the century for social change.

Of course, man being the sort of animal he is, there was no general agreement as to how the ideal state was to be achieved. There was the socialist ideal for the new state, the communist, the anarchist, the Fabian—the list stretches on. And, as with religionists, these reformers were continually at odds both individually and among the groups.

The particular ideology of my sect was socialist and Quaker, two groups then united in the belief that the problem of poverty could be solved by the education of the working man. Not attracted by the theory of revolt of the working class, they wanted to blend the working man into the already existing society by instructing him how to assume a rightful and rewarding place in it.

The movement gained force in the 1870s in England when the University Extension Movement tried to educate workers by establishing extension centers in various cities, and later, in 1899, it reached a peak when Ruskin College was founded at Oxford University. But the extension centers soon became middle class in their turn, and Ruskin College grew hopelessly split over demands by Marxists that only Marxian economics be taught. From then on, the movement began to lose whatever stature it had already achieved.

My mother had become ill in New York a few months after

my father's death—from what was then called a nervous breakdown—and a few days after our arrival in London she entered a sanitarium near Brighton where she was to remain for almost a year.

She had thoroughly disgraced herself aboard ship in the eyes of Sonia and me by taking all her blankets up on deck and sleeping there each night all the way across the Atlantic, even though it was very cold. She couldn't stand the stuffiness of the cabin, she told us, but to us that was a pretty weak excuse. Children of that age are savage social conformists in respect to their elders' conduct.

Although Uncle Senia had invited us to London and had a large house with a staff of servants on the "good" (bourgeois) side of the Crystal Palace, we were soon sent to live with Aunt Mary and Harry Kelly in a small house in a district of London called Penge, on the "bad" (poor) side of the Crystal Palace. The reason was simple: Uncle Senia's wife, Galia, a pleasant woman of formidable formality, simply couldn't stand having two small rambunctious children tearing around her immaculate home.

The Crystal Palace was then a somewhat down-at-the-heels relic of the once flamboyant structure that had been opened for the Great Exhibition of 1851; now it was being used for entertainments such as Buffalo Bill's Wild West Show (which I saw) and for industrial exhibits. It served as an ideal place to dispose of children, and when Senia's children went there, their governess would frequently take us along.

At the Kellys', I was sent to a public school (the counterpart of an American private school) that was distinctly second rate. I can still see myself shambling off every morning in shabby knickers, learning not much more than how to play soccer and to take a rattan caning for displeasing the authorities.

The arrangement lasted only a few months. Neither my sister Sonia nor I were contemplative children. We were activists—I remember my mother telling me how I had scared the wits out of my father, when we were living in Forest Hill, by walking across a railroad trestle over the Passaic River only minutes before a train was scheduled through—

and I imagine we soon wore out our welcome with the Kellys, as we had with the Krimonts. The Kelly house, though not formal, was small.

The Kellys had been connected with the founding of a utopian colony, well known in its day, called Whiteway in the foothills of the Cotswolds of Gloucestershire. At first they thought of sending us to Whiteway, but decided that we were too young. They knew, however, a childless couple, Richard and Mary Hawworth, who lived on a farm a short distance from the colony, and we were sent there to await our mother's recovery.

Actually, my family was connected in one way or another with the founding of three utopian colonies: New Odessa, Whiteway, and a later one at Stelton, New Jersey, near New Brunswick. Founded on the principles of such dreamers as Tolstoi, Kropotkin, and Thoreau, all three played an important, if not overwhelming role in my young life. They had counterparts in Robert Owen's New Harmony Colony in Indiana and Brook Farm in Massachusetts, and resembled some of those being established by young people today. The dream was of a life of natural simplicity, living in accord with nature rather than attempting to master it, combining the nobility of physical labor with, in the case of the colonies I knew, the exaltation of the most sophisticated intellectualism.

In every case, these communes have failed because of a basic perversity in man. Of those communes with which I am most familiar, the pattern of failure was always the same. Everyone started out with the highest of hopes. A group of, say, ten to fifteen families and a varying number of young single persons would pool their resources to buy some land. They would plan a community with several acres for a park, preferably along a brook, on which would be built a combination community hall-schoolhouse-library-double dormitory for the unmarried. Once the community was established, however, the feuding would start. In my colonies, the anarchists feuded with the communists, the Tolstoians with the Kropotkinites, the Mensheviks with the Bolsheviks.

That aside, however, in the England of 1901, Sonia and I

were sent down to live with the Hawworths, near the colony of Whiteway.

I still remember our arrival there.

A magnificent pastoral scene greeted Sonia and me as we walked with Hawworth from Stroud, where the train from London had taken us, to Hawworth's home eight miles away.

The haying season had begun; the mowing machine had not yet come into general use. There were a dozen farm laborers in the fields, their corduroy trousers tied under their knees with multicolored ribbons, colored suspenders over their shirts, brilliant scarves of every description around their necks. One would start down the line of hay, his scythe swinging; the second would let him take two or three strides, then he would start down the next scythe-width of hay, and so on, until there was a whole staggered file of a dozen brilliantly clad men moving down the haying field, swinging in perfect unison like a well-drilled eight-oared crew, stopping at each end to hone their scythes.

Through the summer that Sonia and I lived with the Hawworths, until our mother joined us, I spent most of my time in boredom. There were no children of our age near enough to play with and nothing to do. A farm lay between us and the Whiteway colony. It was a dairy farm owned by a man named William Cawsey, who also traded in cattle. Every Saturday he would journey to Gloucester, ten miles away, to sell cows at auction; led by a horse-drawn cart, the cattle were kept moving by three or four farm laborers armed with switches. The cart was used to carry the laborers back. Frequently I was one of them, and if the high point in your summer is earning a sixpence for chivvying a herd of cows for ten miles, you can imagine what life was like otherwise.

When mother arrived in the fall, much recovered, she stayed with us at the Hawworths' only long enough to find a small cottage at Whiteway colony, and there we moved. Within a few months she had fallen in love with and married one of the three men who were leaders of the colony, a dour and handsome Scot named William Sinclair. Tall and bearded, with enormous drive, and endowed with that indefinable quality of charisma, Sinclair had been a well-to-do bank manager in London until he turned to the dream of utopia. He was endlessly energetic. Once married, he turned to building a house. He was a poor brick maker, however; a year or so later the bricks began to crumble, and the whole house had to be covered with stucco. All through the winter and spring, when I was not going to school or studying, I spent my time running errands for Sinclair.

To illustrate the intellectual climate of Whiteway, however, when Prince Kropotkin once visited the colony, he was stunned to find that both my sister and I had read his classic *Fields, Factories, and Workshops.* "In Russia," he said, "children of your age are still reading fairy tales."

Sinclair, an intellectual snob, became dissatisfied with the education provided at the local school, and at the age of twelve, I was shipped back to London to live with my uncle, John S. Steele, and my aunt, Clara. Steele, the Ulster-born linen shop clerk I had first met in New York, had secured a job as a reporter on the *New York Herald* shortly after we had sailed for London and later, wanting to return to his native British Isles, had gone to work for the London *Daily Express.*

Steele wanted me to attend the St. Paul's Cathedral School (one of whose more distinguished graduates was Viscount Montgomery of Alamein), which provided scholarships for poor boys with voices good enough to sing in the St. Paul's Boys' Choir. Unfortunately for me, my voice already showed signs of changing, and St. Paul's decided that I would be a poor risk. So after a few months of London, it was back to Whiteway.

At this time, in 1905, I began my newspaper career in a very amateurish fashion. For Christmas, my Uncle Jack Steele sent me a hand printing press, and for months thereafter, every two weeks or so, I put out a four-page tabloid on colony doings called *The Whitewayan.*

After one final term in the local school, Sinclair again lost his temper over the school's inadequacies and bluntly informed the school board that he was removing my sister and me from its system. The school board challenged him, and the matter became a *cause célèbre* in the newspapers. It came to the attention of Keir Hardie, the first socialist Labour member of Parliament; and at Hardie's intervention, it was agreed that Sinclair could educate us, provided he could assure the authorities that we *were* being educated. That ended my formal schooling.

What followed was pretty variegated.

First there was Sinclair himself, who thought that education meant quizzing an eleven- and a twelve-year-old on the theories of *Fields, Factories, and Workshops.* Then came listening to the evening discussions among the colonists, who, at varying times, included French, Danish, Dutch, Belgian, Italian, Czech, Russian, Bulgarian, West Indian, Somali, Hindu, Persian, and Zulu. (Most of the blacks were Oxford undergraduates, though the Somali was a stoker who jumped ship from a freighter tied up in London and the Hindu a prince.) The lecture topics included science, philosophy, history, psychology, art, biography, religion, theosophy, spiritualism, Esperanto, and psychoanalysis.

The religious leanings of the colonists ranged from the Society of Friends (the Quakers) to one who was a follower of Zoroaster and a fire worshiper. He was also a bankrupt furrier and was accompanied by a young woman whom he referred to as "my assistant." There was the colonist Francis Sedlak, a Czech rebel, writer, and philosopher, and a devout believer in Tolstoi's "no money" theory—one of the great man's more outrageous pieces of folly. The gist of the theory was that an individual may not use money. The colony itself could because it had to buy staples such as nails and dishes, but not the individual. Postage stamps were excluded in Tolstoi's theory because they represented money, which led Sedlak, on one occasion, to attempt to walk barefoot (he *never* wore shoes) to his publisher in London with an article in the midst of a driving blizzard. He made ten of the eighty miles before even he became aware of the lunacy of this enterprise and turned back.

Finally, for the education of Sonia and me, a "school" was

established at Whiteway, presided over by a Belgian émigré named Gaspard Marin.

Marin was one of that small breed of brilliant, eccentric men of whom the world never hears. A tubercular anarchist (he recovered from the tuberculosis at Whiteway but not the anarchism), he was also a trained ethnologist with an incredible range of learning. He lived at the colony with his wife Jeanne. He later made his way around the world, largely on foot and by bicycle, down through Africa, into India (where he visited Mahatma Gandhi), through Japan, and back through Siberia and Russia.

Robert A. Monson, in his 1931 book *Across Africa on Foot,* describes meeting Marin in Khartoum:

> He was a strange type—a fanatic to judge by his eyes, and a pacifist to judge by his speech and manner. Tanned as brown as the natives amongst whom he had cast his lot, wearing their dress and speaking their tongue, he yet resembled them in nothing else. He told us he was a Belgian by birth and a cosmopolitan by up-bringing—for the twenty-six years prior to his departure from England . . . he had been wandering all over Europe. He was well equipped for the life he had adopted, for he spoke nearly every European language and made a practice of learning any dialect of the people he came amongst. . . . He was a queer fellow—a little mad, perhaps, and yet, maybe, the sanest man alive. It all depends on how one looks at it.

The school he established was conducted more or less on the Socratic principle of the teacher questioning the pupils to establish what was being taught rather than telling them; Marin's lectures were used only to introduce new fields of learning. He taught world culture and French, together with a variety of subjects that occurred to him as he lectured. Sinclair, who was a superb mathematician, taught mathematics; other adults were called in to teach their specialties—world religions, for example. And it worked; the local school authorities professed themselves "confounded" at the range of subjects we were studying.

Those, then, were the elements of my education.

There was another, more practical element. It was at this time that I became actively interested in politics. It had first caught my fancy when I was twelve because of the socialist clubs whose members used to visit the colony and talk of nothing but socialism. At thirteen, I joined the Stroud branch of the Independent Labour Party—socialist—riding my bicycle seven miles each way to attend its meetings, and the next year I became its secretary.

Then, at fifteen, I became campaign manager in my district for Charles Fox, the first Labour candidate to stand for Parliament from a rural constituency. (Keir Hardie had been elected from an industrial coal-mining district.) Fox was a descendant of both George Fox, the seventeenth-century Englishman who founded the Quakers, and of Charles Fox, the eighteenth-century foreign secretary who so bitterly opposed Lord Frederick North's policies toward America, which he correctly foresaw would lead to a rebellion.

My Charles Fox was a Gloucester dentist and another eccentric. A strong, well-built man, very athletic, he wore his hair to his shoulders and affected orthodox Quaker clothes, down to the broad-brimmed Quaker hat and the buckled shoes. He was given to riding around the countryside on his bicycle, lecturing on socialism and holding poetry readings, and he was very well known at Whiteway.

My role in Fox's campaign was to ride around the district on my bicycle, putting up posters, delivering pamphlets, and making the arrangements for rallies. About the only substantive thing I really did was to write a letter to the *Clarion* (the national socialist newspaper) saying that I thought a weakness of the socialists was that they preached only to the already converted and that they distributed their pamphlets only to other socialists; if they would send me some of their pamphlets, I wrote, I would distribute them to farm laborers—those who could read—and to working men. I was convinced, even that early, that it was of vital importance to educate workers about political affairs, which I urged—at my age—to some of the local leaders of the National Agricultural Labourers Union (NALU) whom I met.

The people on the *Clarion* were delighted, and the material poured in, to the disgust of the local postman, who had to pedal it over on his bicycle, and to the irritation of Sinclair, who upbraided me for adding to the postman's burden.

Fox was absolutely crushed in the election, getting only three hundred votes.

In 1910, when I was seventeen, I returned to London to work for my Uncle Jack, who had left the *Express* to become the editor of the Curtis Brown News Bureau. Brown, an American newspaperman, had the idea—a very good one—of forming a bureau to supply feature articles about England to the Sunday supplements of American newspapers, which were then very popular. Brown was to become one of the most famous literary agents in England, and at this particular juncture he was forming his agency, which was why he hired Uncle Jack as editor of his news bureau, and Uncle Jack hired me. It was through Brown's literary agency that I met Lady Gregory, dumpy and unattractive in body though soaring in spirit, and William Butler Yeats, courtly and courteous, with a great mane of flowing hair and a pince-nez. I was paid a pound a week—the family at Whiteway had to stake me to my first long-pants suit—and I lived with Uncle Jack.

Uncle Jack was a superb editor. One of his early features was a series, the first ever, on the Rothschild family which was reprinted almost around the world. My duties were menial. I clipped the British press, did sidelights on the British Parliament—not stories on its actual procedures but features that might be presumed to be of interest to Americans—and interviewed people who also might be of interest to Americans. That job lasted for almost two years, until Brown decided to close his news bureau and devote himself exclusively to the literary-agency business. Uncle Jack went back to the *Express*, and through my own efforts I got my first real bona-fide job, with the *Daily Mirror*.

The *Daily Mirror* was owned by Lord Northcliffe, who, with his brother Lord Rothmere, revolutionized the newspaper business the world around. Among the papers they owned at one time or another were the *Evening News*, the *Daily Mail*, the *Times* of London, and the *Observer*.

The *Mirror* was the prototype of most of today's tabloids. It was, indeed, the first modern tabloid and relied heavily on pictures and feature stories—both preferably offbeat. Pictures came before stories; the photographers were the elite of the staff; the reporters—of whom I was one—their assistants.

It was an absolutely glorious time. To be twenty, on your own in London, working on one of the most famous papers in England, living in a Bohemian world of advanced young men and women—it was heaven.

To add to my euphoria, my first decent assignment was an unqualified success. The Cunard liner *Caronia* had been involved in a collision with a fishing trawler on her way into Southampton. The fishing crew had been rescued, but the *Mirror* sent me to Southampton to see if there were any pictures available. The modus operandi on an assignment like that was the essence of simplicity—you went into the first-class passenger customs shed at Southampton (it's always easier to explain what you want to first-class passengers) and looked for someone carrying a camera.

A lovely American girl who had taken pictures of the rescue operation from the deck of the *Caronia* offered me her entire roll of film, with the stipulation that the *Mirror* develop all the pictures and deliver prints and negatives to her hotel in London. One of the pictures took up almost the entire front page of the next morning's *Mirror*.

My chief value to the *Mirror* was that I could figure angles to stories, the offbeat slant that the paper wanted. Once, a distinguished art authority had delivered a lecture arguing that the statue of the Venus de Milo in the Louvre represented the ideal of female beauty. I suggested that the paper sponsor a contest to find a girl in England whose measurements most closely approximated the Venus's, and the paper did—not without a certain amount of trouble, which added naturally, to the publicity. In the first place, the Venus's measurements were not available, and the authorities at the Louvre were averse to our taking them. We actually had to ask the Foreign Office to make an official request of the French government to obtain them. Then, although I was traveling in advanced circles, the *Mirror* editors weren't, and we had to work out an elaborate system for measuring the girl contestants in privacy —this was long before bathing-beauty contests had become familiar, of course—by women measurers, and the winner had to be photographed through gauze. An interesting feature of the contest was that although we found a dozen or so girls with the bust, waist, and hip measurements, not one could match the slenderness of the Venus's eight-inch ankle.

I worked on the *Mirror* about two years, being assigned the sort of stories that most reporters cover—fires, accidents, disturbances. Those were the days of demonstrations over Irish independence and women's suffrage. Quite by accident, I was at Epsom Downs—with an inspector from Scotland Yard to do a story on how the Yard spotted pickpockets—on Derby Day in 1913 when Emily Davidson, a leading figure in the "Militant Movement for Women's Suffrage," ran out onto the course as the Derby was being run and was killed by the horses.

The investiture of Charles as Prince of Wales in 1969 reminded me again of how some things seem never to change. The American newspapers and magazines were full of stories about the difficulties of covering the ceremonies because Caernarvon Castle, where the investiture is always held, is really a thirteenth-century fortress, bare of the amenities that modern reporters regard as their due, such as telephone facilities and men's rooms. I remembered myself there in 1911 when Edward VIII was made Prince of Wales, feeling exactly the same way, waiting outside the castle walls until the *Mirror* photographer could make his way out of the castle keep to the wall to drop his plates down to me.

My career at the *Mirror* ended abruptly. Northcliffe one day simply decided that his staff was too big, and about half of the younger reporters were fired overnight, a common practice that lasted until well into the 1930s when the British

National Union of Journalists (in America, the American Newspaper Guild) began to gain power. I was a member of the British union—in which the brightest star was H. G. Wells—but much good it did me. I was out of a job.

My Uncle Jack now got me a job on the *Daily Express*, which I remember chiefly because the *Express* required its reporters, if they were covering a formal evening affair, to wear a proper dinner jacket. At the time I resented the outlay of money, but I wore it for thirty years, so I guess it was worth it.

Uncle Jack went on to become London correspondent and one of the top war correspondents for the *Chicago Tribune*. (His first war was the Boer War, when he became friendly with Sir Winston Churchill, and his last was World War II.) When he died in 1951, he was European manager for the *Tribune*.

It was while I was on the *Express* that I decided I wanted to be more than a reporter. It was exciting, but when you are twenty-two, you know you want to do more with your life than write about the doings of pickpockets at Epsom Downs and run contests to see which young woman has a thirty-seven-inch bust.

So after a few months on the *Express*, I left to go to work for the *Daily Herald*, the new editor of which was George Lansbury. (In 1922, the *Herald* was to become the official paper of the British Labour Party.) Lansbury had begun his working life as a checker on the Great Eastern Railway, had become a Liberal politician, then a socialist, and had been elected to Parliament from Bow in 1910.

While working on the *Herald*, I found myself in the most turbulent period of my young manhood.

My whole world seemed filled with problems. Some of them were due simply to the natural process of growing up. I had, for example, become completely disillusioned with the commune way of life in which I had been raised. I had come to view it simply as a way of escape from the real world, which was perfectly all right, as far as I was concerned, for a man like Sinclair. He had lived in the world of London, and if he wanted to retire to the world of the Cotswolds and live by his own physical labor, that was his privilege. But the theories of the commune had no larger meaning for me. One of the basic concepts—that of each member contributing to the welfare of the colony according to his ability—had been tried and found wanting at Whiteway. The colony had been confronted with the basic fact that some people are industrious and some are lazy; some are honest and some are thieves. When the industrious people at Whiteway discovered they were being taken advantage of, and when the honest people found that they were being victimized by pilferers, they reluctantly—and after the interminable discussions that were a concomitant of life there—abandoned that principle of communal living. So I had come to realize that this sort of life was not for me, but I did not know precisely what sort of world should be formed and what I should do to help shape it.

Another problem—more vexing for someone who is twenty-two—was that I had fallen desperately in love with a stunning redhead named Gertrude Ennis. She was a Roman Catholic —unfortunately, to my way of thinking—and if I was to marry her, I would have to join her church. As a thoroughgoing agnostic with a tendency toward atheism in moments of despair, I could not envision myself joining the Roman Catholic church without becoming the most detectable liar since Ananias.

Both problems—what sort of world I wanted and my unhappy love affair—were not so much solved for me as ended by the stage having been set for World War I. The slaughter was about to begin.

The memories of the months from mid-1914 until March of 1916, when I returned to the United States, tumble about in my mind. I have read a number of histories of the events that led to World War I and almost as many about the early months of the war itself, and I think that I have a fair intellectual grasp of the forces in play, the cross-purposes and cross-ambitions of those involved, the events that took place. None of that has any relationship to how I felt, or how I feel when I think back.

What I first remember is the weather. England has never had, I think, two summers as lovely as those of 1914 and 1915: almost endless, glorious golden days, the sun shining, the sky a flawless blue, the incredible British gardens a profusion of ordered brilliance.

I remember next how isolated we seemed from what was happening. It is impossible to exaggerate the contrast with today. The newspapers were filled with stories of the war, but there was neither television nor radio; there were no news magazines nor picture magazines as we know them now. Our "illustrated journals" paid due attention to the blood-drenched conflict but generally with pictures of Lady So-and-So in her new Red Cross uniform, some of our "brave boys" having coffee and doughnuts at a mobile canteen, or Captain Radclyffe-Jones, glittering with polish, lounging against the wing of his Handley Page bombing plane. There was none of today's incessant bombardment of news of every military action, none of the endless publication of the most savage of war pictures for which today's mass media compete.

Not that we did not realize there was a war going on. Far from it. Especially by the summer of 1915, the casualty figures had begun to mount as if there would be no end. Mons and Ypres had already been fought; 1916 would bring the two battles of the Somme and still ahead the unbelievable, incomprehensible carnage of Passchendaele, Vimy, Cambrai, and Verdun.

I also remember the savagery of the British people at war. I had never seen anything like it before, nor have I since. Overnight, the country was filled with a seething hatred of Germany and everything German, all the more astounding since every British schoolboy knew that von Blücher and his Prussians had fought by the side of Wellington at Waterloo, and the name of their own Royal House was Saxe-Coburg-Gotha. All that changed in a flash; everything that even sounded Germanic was suspect. I myself was turned down by the British armed forces simply because of my Germanic name. George V changed the name of his House to Windsor; the Bismarck Hotel in London became the Dorchester.

I remember very clearly how I learned about the beginning of the war. I had gone down to Whiteway, and my redheaded Irish charmer had come from London to spend part of her vacation there. Although we read the newspapers avidly, we had quite forgotten that the following Monday would be a bank holiday. The actual movement of troops that made the war inevitable—as the Kaiser said later in his memoirs, "to his boundless dismay"—had begun on Saturday. So, on Monday, all unknowing, we decided on a picnic.

I can still see today the exact spot we chose. It lay about three miles from our house, through paths in the woods into a stunning, beautiful glade of at least ten acres. Unspoiled, untouched, lovely. Nothing could have been more delightful. Gertrude had brought down a paperback edition of one of Shaw's new plays called *The Shewing Up of Blanco Posnet.* After we all had eaten and were lying on the grass, I read the whole play aloud. Then we had tea and slowly meandered our way homeward through the beautiful afternoon.

In our kitchen, hot, dusty, tired, and trembling, sat the old teachers of the Whiteway School, Gaspard and Jeanne Marin, their knapsacks lying on the floor. They were appalled at our gay and carefree faces. I will never forget Gaspard's exact words.

"All Europe is in flames!" he cried, and broke into tears.

So it was.

Shortly afterward, I had to leave the *Herald* because every able-bodied young man not in the service had to be employed in work vital to the war effort. I went back to Whiteway to do farm work, but after a few weeks I left.

Restless, first of all, I wanted to get away. Frustrated by my own beliefs—a pacifist and a socialist in a country at war—frustrated in love, I had reached a point where I could barely stand my stepfather, Sinclair. It is one thing to read about a man who has purpose, drive, and charisma and quite another to live with him. I found him a fanatic, utterly convinced that everything he believed, including the necessity of twelve hours hard physical labor every day, was correct and true. People who didn't believe as he did were fools. He was impossible.

I decided that the thing for me to do was to see more of England. By now I'd been there almost fourteen years, and I'd seen nothing (outside of a few journalistic trips) except London and the Cotswolds. So I simply set off on foot.

The first job that I got was with a brute of a dairy-and-sheep farmer in Leicestershire—that part of England that is real fox-hunting country, big estates, wide flat fields, and few of the stone walls that they have in the Cotswolds. That was where I had my first experience in shearing sheep. Shearing sheep, you may take my word for it, is not an occupation for gentlemen. No matter how well they're held, sheep kick; the grease and oil on the wool works its way into your hands, your clothes, your very skin; and after a time the stench becomes literally unbearable. You just have to stop, go off, and breathe some air.

From Leicestershire I journeyed—at the suggestion of some of my Quaker friends—to a farm in the West Riding section of Yorkshire.

A strange memory remains of the farm in West Riding. It was poor farming country, broken up by tiny villages, almost every one of which had a wool- or worsted-manufacturing plant. (The milk from our farm, for example, traveled early every morning by train to Huddersfield, which called itself "the capital of the wool industry.") The village near our farm had a small woolen mill where the morning shift started at six o'clock. British mill workers in those days wore wooden clogs as they walked over the cobbled streets to the mills, and the clatter of the clogs reverberating on the morning air through the surrounding hills and valleys carried for miles.

On our farm, if you missed waking up on time, the first thing you would hear would be the sound of the clogs, well over a mile away, echoing into your window.

After some months of farm work and my first real venture into labor union activity—trying to help organize farm workers into the NALU—I began to change again. Part of it, I think, was due to the casualty lists, the killing of what Rupert Brooke called "golden youth." I don't think there was a person, or certainly a family, in England who didn't have someone, or know someone, on a casualty list. A good friend of mine in London, who had worked with me in the movement for women's suffrage, had been killed in the fourth month of the war. I wanted to participate in it, to help stop it, but because of my name, I couldn't. As a further complication, I had at this time decided that I wanted to return to America.

There is no completely rational way to explain this decision. My mother and stepfather thought that I had gone mad. They themselves had no intention of leaving Whiteway. And in the middle of wartime it was not the simplest thing in the world to get from England to America. But I was determined to go back. What ties, what bonds drew me there—I had none, really—I don't know. I was just going.

Chapter Three

FINDING PASSAGE on a ship to the United States in 1916 was not as difficult a problem as I had imagined. The rush of those Americans trapped in Europe by the outbreak of the war to return to their homes had ended a year previous, and even though the sinking of the *Lusitania* a year earlier was still fresh in everyone's mind, unrestricted submarine warfare was not to begin for some months. My major problem was obtaining a passport.

When my mother had brought Sonia and me to England, passports did not exist (shades of the Victorian era!), but now they did—and my mother had no copy of my birth certificate. No amount of writing to the municipal authorities in Forest Hills, New Jersey, was able to produce one, so I had to go about the tedious process of proving that I had, indeed, been born in the United States.

Harry Kelly was in the United States at this time, and he was able to round up a dossier of notarized statements from relatives and friends of my father and mother testifying to my birth. In London, a good friend of my stepfather's, the liberal

Labour lawyer Gilbert Roe took the dossier to the then US Ambassador to the Court of St. James's, Walter Hines Page, (Roe and Page also were friends of many years standing), and eventually I was granted a passport.

Instead of going directly to Liverpool to board ship—transatlantic passenger ships were no longer sailing from Southampton to the United States; they were sailing from Liverpool and around the north of Ireland to avoid the submarines—I returned to London to say good-by to the Steeles and Gertrude Ennis.

Leaving my mother, sister, and stepfather had been difficult enough, the Steeles almost as much so, but saying good-by to Gertrude was the most painful of all. Our parting was drenched in that end-of-the-world sentimental romanticism of the young. We had dinner in Soho and then went to "La Bohème," conducted by Sir Henry Beecham, with a British cast. (It was very fashionable then for the British to present French and Italian operas.) Gertrude accompanied me to King's Cross Station, where I was to get the overnight train to Liverpool.

The station was dark and gloomy, filled with smoke and steam, busier than it ever would have been at that hour in peacetime, crowded with soldiers, and our goody-bys were as tearful and kiss-laden as all the wartime good-bys between lovers since war and love have existed.

I boarded the train, as miserable as I can ever remember feeling, my heart wretched, my mind assailed with increasing doubts about my decision.

Liverpool the next morning did little to cheer me up. At its sunniest Liverpool never strikes me as a carefree place, and this morning was raw and dreary. In addition, I had to undergo a long examination by a security officer who wanted to examine every detail of my life, with particular emphasis on why I was leaving England to go to the United States. I had a pretty standard British accent in those days, and my having an American passport seemed to arouse suspicion in the mind of the security officer. Also, I was wearing a small red lapel button in the shape of a hand—the emblem of the Irish Transport Workers' Union, which had been presented to me by James Larkin, the Irish trade unionist who headed the Transport Workers and whom I had met while working for the *Herald.*

The trip across the Atlantic in winter, on a blacked-out and nearly passengerless liner, was illuminated for me only by a spirit of adventure, the element of danger. I was returning to my native land about as ignorant of it as the rawest immigrant.

It was a cold and misty morning when the ship moved into New York Harbor. The sun, trying to burn through the clouds, imparted a strange and eerie look to the top stories of the skyscrapers, visible above the layers of fog and mist. An unnatural pink tint permeated the whole gray sky. The world looked exactly as Maxfield Parrish or Burne-Jones might have painted it.

A goodly number of my relatives around New York had gathered at the pier to welcome me. It was a gay and festive meeting that did a great deal to revive my spirits.

They were further revived as the mist began to clear, blown away by the wind that had begun to spring up. New York began to look so bright and clean, so cheerful and colorful and carefree that I could feel myself responding to the whole atmosphere. I had a tremendous sense of having arrived in a fresher climate than that of England, of having come to a more exciting world in which to live and work.

My first days back in the States were wonderful. I was staying with the Kisliks. (Mrs. Kislik was my Aunt Sophie, my mother's eldest sister.) Alexander Kislik, the ex-New Odessa colonist she had married, had become a fairly wealthy businessman, and I was treated royally: sightseeing trips around New York, attending the theater, dinners at the better New York restaurants, visiting with the seemingly innumerable Krimonts, their in-laws, families, and friends.

It was only slowly, after the first weeks, that I was struck with the realization that, to all intents and purposes, in my native land I was an immigrant.

I had left the United States when I was seven, and I was

now twenty-three. I wore British clothes, I spoke with a British accent—which Americans were inclined to think was an affectation—and most of all, I *thought* like a Britisher.

We are all products of our own cultures, of course—I think that the true mark of genius is the capacity to transcend one's own culture—and nothing impressed that upon me as much as my first weeks back in the United States. Except for speaking the same language after a fashion, America was as foreign to me as Spain. The newspapers were different, the customs of everyday living were different (no tea), even the side of the street one drove on and the side of the pavement one walked on were different. (And it wasn't even called a pavement. It was called a sidewalk.) In addition to such surface considerations, I found myself the victim of a whole series of conflicting emotional and intellectual values.

The Kislik family with whom I was living, for example, was pretty worldly-success-minded; other families, also relatives, were radicals. But the radical movement in the States at that time, as I found it, was so confused that I could make neither head nor tail of it. In England, even the working-class people had some degree of political sophistication. They knew the difference between a communist and a socialist. In America, even writers and political lecturers didn't seem to know the difference. More than that, the American radical group itself seemed to be split into so many small feuding factions that it didn't take much political acumen on my part to diagnose why it was so totally ineffectual.

Moreover, I wasn't able to grasp the mood of the people. In England, it was easy for me to define how people felt—about business, about politics, about the war. In the United States, I could get none of that feeling. The economic scene seemed stratified into the two layers of capital and labor, politics seemed stratified into Republicans and Democrats, and as far as the war was concerned, America seemed peculiarly amorphous. People were anti-German, not quite as frenetic as the British, but not far removed from it; pro-Ally, but still convinced that America should "avoid foreign entanglements," that Europeans should "fight it out among themselves," and that the United States really shouldn't get involved.

I had a job: my mother's youngest brother, Arnold Krimont, already following the capitalist tradition of that part of the family, was running a successful scrap-metal business in Harlem, and he hired me as a checker of trucks unloading in his yards.

In my free time, I drifted around, visiting libraries, museums, art galleries, trying to get the feel of the city, trying to comprehend its vivid spectacle, so different from London. One of my young Krimont cousins attended a branch of City College in the Bronx, and I spent some time with him, almost flabbergasted at the difference between City College and Oxford or Cambridge, and also trying to understand such American sports as baseball and football.

After a few months, this sort of existence began to pall on me, and I decided that I had better get a real job and go to work. All I knew, of course, was newspapering, and I applied at an agency—no longer in existence, the old Fernald Agency—that specialized in finding jobs for newspapermen. I wasn't confident of getting a job because my first few months in New York had taught me that American newpapers were much different from British ones, much less sophisticated, even the best of them.

I had told the Fernald Agency that I had done drama reviews and knew a good deal about the (British) stage, something about music, and that I had written countless stories for London papers. I had already decided that I had no hope at all of finding employment with a New York City newspaper, but I was overjoyed to find that the *Springfield* (Mass.) *Republican* had a job open as Sunday editor.

The *Republican* was a famous paper in those days, although, like so many before and after, it took advantage of its reputation by paying its editorial employees a bare living wage. The craft unions had a more realistic point of view: You paid the printer the going wage, whatever your reputation. But as far as editorial employees were concerned, it was supposed to be an "honor" to work for the *Republican,* and the Sunday editor's salary was to be twenty-five dollars a week.

I remember my first trip from New York to Springfield, via train, to be interviewed for the job. My first trip into the countryside of the United States, away from New York, is still almost as clear as my first vision of Stroud in England. It was early summer, and the train wound its way up the valley of the Connecticut River. I could see from the train window the fields of tobacco stretching into the distance, from just beyond Hartford almost to Springfield, each field covered with what seemed like acres of cheesecloth stretched taut on poles that kept it about ten feet above the tobacco (to ward off direct rays of the sun). The image of the fields marching away from me, the vast rectangles of cotton cloth interspersed with the thin lines of growing tobacco, and the pattern of winding roads going up the hillside left an ineradicable impression.

My interview was with Edward Hooker, the managing editor and publisher of the *Republican*—a very tall man, gaunt and craggy, the very image of a New Englander—whose family owned the paper. The interview didn't go too well at the start, I felt. There was the matter of my British accent and my British clothes, my lack of formal education, and my generally spotty background, but as the interview wore on it seemed to me that Hooker became warmer.

Nonetheless, I took the train back to New York very much of two minds as to whether I would be hired. Hooker told me later that he too had many doubts, but that finally, late that afternoon, he sat down at his desk and wrote me a letter offering me the job.

I received Hooker's letter the next day and immediately said my good-bys to the Krimont family, packed all my belongings into two suitcases, and took the next day's train back to Springfield.

I was able to find a furnished room in a small boarding house, close enough to the *Republican* to be able to walk to work, with a kind landlady who would give breakfast and, for a modest fee, do most of my laundry.

It was a busy life in which I found myself. Actually, despite my title of "Sunday Editor," it turned out that basically I was the drama editor. Springfield was one of the renowned provincial theatrical cities of the day. Tryouts for Broadway shows were often held there and it had a very good repertory company of its own. While I was there, such luminaries as Harry Lauder and Victor Herbert made special appearances. A good part of the Sunday edition (apart from the news sections, with which I was not involved) was devoted to the theater section. It was nothing for me (no young man then thought anything of it) to work sixty hours a week. For recreation there was riding trolley cars, something no longer possible. Then, before the overwhelming ubiquity of the automobile and the bus, trolley cars linked all the towns of the Connecticut Valley. It was an almost perfect form of transportation—cheap, convenient, fun, and a magnificent way to see the country.

Of all the people I met on the paper, by all odds the one who was to turn out to be most important to me was a man named August Lardy, for Lardy introduced me to the girl I was to marry. Lardy fancied himself a radical, though his radicalism mostly consisted of denouncing capitalism in social conversations with his friends, expounding on the virtues of free love, and going to socialist and radical meetings.

After Lardy left the *Republican* and went to work for the *Boston American,* we kept in touch. I would go to Boston two or three times a month, mostly to attend the theater, and I generally would telephone him. A couple of times he had mentioned a girl named Kate Van Eaton, who seemed very much to have captured his fancy. It was on the Easter weekend of 1918, when I was visiting Boston, that I called Lardy, and he asked me if I would like to have lunch at a restaurant called Boni's on Sunday with him and Kate Van Eaton. I agreed.

Kate Van Eaton had rebelled against both her family and her background. I found later that her family traced back much further than either branch of mine, not that it mattered much to me. (Van Eaton, it turned out, was a simplification of Van Etten—Etten is a small town in Holland—and the family records stretched to the baptismal lines of Jacobus Jensen van Etten in the town hall of Etten in 1654. Jacobus emigrated to America around 1656.) At the time, however, I learned only that she came from Xenia, Ohio, where her family were strait-laced farmers, ironclad conservative Republicans, strict Presbyterians, and teetotalers. Kate had been graduated from Wellesley College in 1916, a time when just for an Ohio farm girl to go to Wellesley was no small feat of rebellion in itself. She was a social worker at Denison House, a settlement house in Boston, and very much of an anarchist—at least theoretically.

I won't say that I fell in love with Kate at first sight, but she was certainly handsome (not pretty in the conventional sense), intelligent, and stimulating, and we had what I thought was a fine lunch in all ways. The food was superb, the company was enlivening, the day was sparkling, and after lunch we walked around Boston Common.

The next day, Easter Monday, was also a holiday, and the program was repeated—lunch, a walk around the Common, then a longer walk along the Esplanade beside the Charles River.

I had to return to Springfield that night, and the next day I sent Kate a copy of one of Oscar Wilde's collection of fairy tales, *The House of Pomegranates*, along with a rather longish letter telling her how delightful her company was.

She wrote back to thank me and to mention, quite incidentally, that in mid-May she was going to visit the campuses of Smith College in Northampton, Massachusetts, and Mount Holyoke College in South Hadley, about twenty miles from Springfield, to talk to seniors about the importance of working in settlement houses. The train from Boston to Northampton stops in Springfield. Naturally, I arranged to meet her.

I shall not detail my courtship of Kate. Like every young man, I arranged to meet her whenever I could and sweet-talked her to the best of my ability. My best laid plans went astray, however, because of a new development in my life.

I received notification that I was to be drafted into the United States Army.

This posed for me that same dilemma that I had experienced in England. Here I was, still a pacifist, probably far more aware than most Americans of the extent of the slaughter in Europe. The top generals might have known in the summer of 1918 that the war had turned in favor of the Allies (historians, too, could explain it clearly afterward), but to me, the average individual, the fighting raged on, the casualties continued, Ludendorff had launched a new offensive in the West.

What was I to do—claim status as a pacifist (I knew my family in England would morally disown me if I did not) or go into the army?

Even today, in my own mind, I'm not sure of all the factors that influenced my decision. Was it because I was still convinced that, pacifism or not, the Germans had to be halted? Was it because of the memory of all the "shining young men" I knew who had been killed and with whom I felt an obscure brotherhood? Was it because I suddenly realized that America was my native land and I wanted to serve her cause?

Whatever the reasons, with the dire predictions of some of my friends in my mind that the war could go on forever, I reported for induction and was shipped off to Camp Devens for training.

After all my soul-searching, I wish I could report that I attained some sort of military distinction. I didn't. In basic training I qualified as expert with the old Springfield rifle; I was promoted to private first class; I was put in charge of the camp entertainment unit because of my connection with the theater and helped stage a moderately elaborate (for an army camp) version of a great Broadway hit musical of the day, *Chu Chin Chow*. Before my contingent was ready to be shipped overseas, the armistice came, and I was discharged.

I had, of course, been seeing Kate as often as I could during those months—which was none too frequently—and by the time the war ended, we knew that we were deeply in love.

I felt, however, that before we got married, I ought to have a job. When I was discharged, the *Republican* told me that—despite their patriotic promises when I had left—in my absence they had hired a new Sunday editor and had no need for my services. Discharged servicemen had no right to their former jobs in those days.

There was no choice except to return to New York and look for work. Kate, meanwhile, had left her job at Denison House to work for the Bureau of Labor Statistics (BLS).

Having become disillusioned with the "minor palliatives," as she put it, that social workers offered the poor, she had concluded that only federal legislative action could solve the problem of poverty. But in order to get federal legislators to move, you had to have incontrovertible evidence that your case was correct.

Basically, her job at BLS was to go into the field to gather the statistics that would be correlated into the bureau's report. This meant that I was seeing her even less frequently than I had when I was on the *Republican* or in the army.

In New York, rather than impose on the Kisliks again, I stayed this time with the Krimonts, the more radical branch of the family. While looking for a job, I fell into the habit of attending all sorts of radical meetings, where I met an anarchist, Emma Goldman; a communist, Louis Budenz; a socialist, Norman Thomas; and a plain old-fashioned liberal, Roger Baldwin. Of the four, I got along best with Thomas and Baldwin. Whatever their political differences, they were reasonable men. I liked Budenz personally and admired his unceasing energy, but he was so relentlessly a communist and so adamantly a dialectician that it was impossible for me to talk politics with him. It was the same with Emma Goldman. To both her and Budenz the world was divided into the good and the bad. What they believed in was good; the rest was bad. The real difference between them was that Emma Goldman considered communists to be spineless political weaklings only a little better than capitalists; Budenz thought that anarchists were totally ignorant of the politics of the human animal and of the structure of government.

The job I finally took was not one designed to advance my career. It came through the Krimonts, and it was as acting principal of The Modern School at the third of the utopian colonies that my family had had a hand in founding—at Stelton, New Jersey. About fifty families had chipped in to buy some ninety acres of farmland there, and while it soon followed the path of both New Odessa and Whiteway, it did have the distinction of housing The Modern School, one of the very first progressive schools founded in the United States.

I say "housing" because the school was actually founded in New York City (Emma Goldman, who couldn't stand children, was one of the founders), but then it had to move, and to Stelton it went. This was the only reason the job of acting principal was open. The first principal was Will Durant, and when the school moved, he refused to do so.

On the strength of my new job, I very much wanted Kate to marry me immediately, but complications with her work made it impossible. Finally, in New York City one Saturday morning, April 26, 1920, we decided to marry on the spur of the moment. We found a policeman on the street and asked him where we could get married. He directed us to City Hall. We got a license and were married half an hour later.

We went back to the small apartment where she was staying with two old college classmates; she was to pack her belongings. I then went to Penn Station to catch the next train back to Stelton to make ready her new home (two rooms).

I was under no illusion that I could fill Will Durant's shoes as principal, and neither were the directors of The Modern School. The curriculum of the school had been set, the teachers perfectly qualified to follow it. All of them, in fact, were more qualified than I. I did have one talent, however, that the directors wanted: I knew a good deal about the theater. I had produced shows in the army and at Whiteway, I was a passable actor—an amateur, of course—and I was passionately interested in the theater. The school thought that I would be the ideal man to take over the drama program.

More important, the school needed a fund raiser. (Such schools always do.) Naturally, it looked to progressive groups and individuals for money, and the directors thought that my background—England, intellectualism, socialism, political campaign worker—qualified me for this function.

When Kate arrived at Stelton, she was immediately hired as a teacher, and for a few months we led the blissful existence of a pair of newlywed idealists. Kate was teaching at a school that was a model of its kind. I was teaching the craft of the theater (including staging some pretty good juvenile productions) and calling on New Jersey and New York trade-union officials to solicit funds for the school. This was my first real contact with officials of the organized trade-union movement in the United States, with men who were to be so important in my life later on.

But, after these first few idyllic months, the directors of The Modern School hired Alexis and Elizabeth Ferm to direct the school. They arrived in early summer, a highhanded and autocratic pair who immediately made it clear to Kate and me that they were the experts on progressive child education and we a pair of bungling amateurs. This did not particularly distress me since I had never made any pretense at being an educator, but I resented it for Kate because she really was a superb teacher of young children.

While I was stewing with this resentment, Roger Baldwin called me to say that B. W. Huebsch, then America's most important avant-garde publisher, wanted a man as his advertising and publicity director. S. N. Behrman, who had held the job, had resigned to devote all his efforts to writing plays. I was overjoyed. Huebsch (his firm was eventually incorporated into Viking Press) was publishing the works of Thorstein Veblen, Aldous Huxley, James Joyce, D. H. Lawrence, and Sherwood Anderson, as well as a literary magazine, the *Freeman*. So, with pleasure, I resigned from The Modern School.

For almost two years I commuted every workday from Stelton to the Huebsch offices in New York. The commuting was partly because Kate was still teaching at Stelton, despite the Ferms, but largely because it was much cheaper to continue to live at Stelton rather than rent an apartment in New

York for Kate, me, and, as of April 1921, our first-born daughter, Alison.

The Huebsch job was exciting—just getting to know Anderson was stimulating—but like all good things, it came to an end. In mid-1924, the woman who had been financing Huebsch withdrew her support. She was Mrs. Frances Neilson, daughter of Gustavus Swift, founder of the Swift Packing Company and wife of a moderately well-known British playwright. Why she withdrew her support, I will never know—she certainly never expected to make money from the enterprise. Again, I was out of a job.

At this point, walking down the street one day in Newark, I ran into Louis Budenz. Budenz had become the New Jersey campaign manager for the presidential drive of Sen. Robert A. LaFollette of Wisconsin, running on the Progressive ticket. A group of unions in Pennsylvania, principally the railroad unions, had established a campaign fund for LaFollette in Pennsylvania. These unions wanted a man to run LaFollette's campaign in that state for them. Louis told me that he thought I should take the job, thankless as it might seem. (Calvin Coolidge was running against John W. Davis that year; Coolidge looked to be, and was, a shoo-in). Louis offered to introduce me to James H. Maurer, then president of the Pennsylvania State Federation of Labor and the man who would choose the campaign manager.

I felt that the job would be useful and exciting, and the pay would be twenty-five dollars a week, plus reasonable expenses.

It *was* useful and exciting, in more ways than I can enumerate. While I knew that LaFollette wasn't going to win, I still had the opportunity of meeting the great man. In addition, I met many of the labor leaders in Pennsylvania, and I gained a good deal of political experience. LaFollette's campaign was much more sophisticated than Charles Fox's in England, for which I had worked, and I learned much more about how political campaigns were run, which was to stand me in great stead later. I learned about organizing an American political campaign—the thousand-and-one details of working out schedules, arranging for public appearances, calling local chairmen, deciding on the "honored guest" list, choosing introductory speakers, all the paraphernalia of a campaign. I became so involved in the campaign that, although my son John Arnold was born in August of that year, I don't think that I saw him or Kate more than ten times before the end of the campaign. I did so much traveling within a period of six weeks that the campaign is a blur in my mind, but during it I discovered that I was an effective, if low-keyed, public speaker.

My greatest disappointment of the campaign was that, after it was over, the labor political organization that had been constructed to run it simply fell apart. No amount of talk on my part, or anyone else's, could persuade the Pennsylvania union leadership to continue their political work.

On the day after election, of course, I was again out of a job. By this time, though, I was sufficiently well known in the Pennsylvania-New Jersey area that I was told of an opening on the Camden, New Jersey, *Post Telegram*, for a telegraph editor. I held the job until February 1926, when J. David Stern, the owner of the rival paper, the *Courier*, bought the *Post Telegram*.

Stern, later publisher of the *Philadelphia Record* and the first major publisher in America to sign a contract with the American Newspaper Guild, had a reputation as a "liberal" publisher, but I had a totally different view of him. When he incorporated the *Post Telegram* into the *Courier*, he fired the entire *Post Telegram* editorial staff out of hand.

Kate was now expecting our third child, and I was *again* without a job.

At this time, James Maurer, who had hired me to run the LaFollette campaign in Pennsylvania, asked me to do a writing job for Gifford Pinchot, then governor of Pennsylvania and a great friend of Maurer's.

Pinchot was one of the most dedicated public servants in American history. A pioneer conservationist, he established what is today the US Forest Service; under his leadership Pennsylvania was the first state in the union to provide a fund for old-age pensions. At this time a Viennese refugee named Abraham Epstein worked for Pinchot, preparing the report on old-age pensions. Epstein was a brilliant man, but his English was atrocious. I was hired to cast his report into comprehensible language.

While I was still working on the report, in the fall of 1926 (my younger daughter Anne had been born in July), I was asked to become the campaign director for a slate of socialist candidates running for office in Reading, from mayor on down. The campaign was heavily supported by the American Federation of Full-Fashioned Hosiery Workers, who were engaged in an all-out campaign to organize the mill workers in and around Reading. During the campaign, the union, the strongest subsidiary of the parent United Textile Workers Union (UTWU), told me that they had decided to establish the post of public relations and research director at their headquarters in Philadelphia and offered it to me. I agreed, and so, almost without realizing it, I had finally embarked on my lifetime career in the American labor movement.

Chapter Four

WHATEVER I HAD expected of my new job as research director and chief of public relations for the Hosiery Workers, I was not prepared to be, within a relatively few months, precipitated into the middle of one of the most bitter, violence-ridden strikes in the history of the American labor movement. I discovered that it was one thing to read about guns and to fire one on a target range in the army; it was quite another to see a man ten feet away with a loaded rifle, perfectly willing to shoot.

This was the Bemberg-Glanzstoff strike at Elizabethton, Tennessee.

Bemberg-Glanzstoff was a German firm that had been lured to the South shortly after World War I by all the blandishments that could be offered to industry: cheap labor, cheap power, and cheap taxes. The Southern campaign to attract industry had begun before World War I, aimed first at United States firms. It had been particularly successful in the New England textile industry. The campaign had been of ever-increasing concern to people in organized labor, especially the sector involved with textiles, because the basis of the South's cheap labor pool was total and violent anti-unionism.

Against that background, Bemberg-Glanzstoff, one of the earliest companies to capitalize on the use of rayon thread for textiles, had built two plants within a few miles of each other at Elizabethton and had set up two separate American companies to operate them, one called American Bemberg, the other American Glanzstoff.

A whole series of factors led to the Bemberg-Glanzstoff strike. First, by 1928, long before the real Depression, the textile industry was seriously ailing. American manufacturers had been hurt by competition from abroad, by the wartime expansion that had led to overproduction, by the introduction of new fibers, even by style changes. Women particularly were wearing fewer clothes than they had a generation earlier, and skimpier ones in the bargain; short skirts were the making of the full-fashioned hosiery industry, but they threatened to ruin textile manufacturers who made cloth for skirts and dresses.

Manufacturers tried to overcome their problems by lowering costs and by increasing production even more. For mill workers, this meant the "stretchout"—fewer men and women working longer hours to keep the same number of looms producing even more cloth. Twelve-hour workdays were common, as was the seventy-two-hour work week. Children and women, the cheapest possible labor, were assigned to night shifts. And the wages! At Bemberg-Glanzstoff, one woman supervisor, with fifty-two girls working under her, was paid $10.18 a week.

Bemberg-Glanzstoff had an additional problem in Elizabethton that they had not foreseen. In Germany, they had been accustomed to dealing with old-time industrial workers who knew what factory life was like. In Elizabethton, they were dealing with back-country Scotch-Irish mountain folk who had never seen a piece of machinery more complicated than a Model-T Ford. In addition, their looms were spinning rayon. Rayon spinning is a much more technical and difficult process than silk spinning. Silk is a natural fiber, and the temperature in a silk mill can vary by four or five degrees without damage to the thread. In a rayon plant, a temperature change of as much as two degrees spells disaster. And in those early days rayon thread itself had not been perfected. A sort of slime from it would build up on the looms and gradually slow them down.

There were also endless mechanical problems with the new machines, and this exacerbated the feelings of the Bemberg-Glanzstoff workers, since they were not paid while a machine was not working. Moreover, the new plants had no facilities for feeding workers, which became a major issue; and housing was extremely scarce and very expensive.

All in all, Bemberg-Glanzstoff was ripe for a strike.

The way the strike began was the essence of simplicity. The women in the plant simply walked off their jobs. They had no union, and they held no meetings. They had simply talked among themselves, decided that wages and working conditions were intolerable, and one fine day just quit. Like that.

At first, the management considered their departure a sort of joke that would soon end, but after a few days, with production remaining at a standstill, Bemberg-Glanzstoff decided that the problem was serious. The company went into court and got an injunction against the workers.

Meanwhile, the climate of Elizabethton was changing. The townspeople—even those who at first had been strong supporters of "bringing in industry"—were beginning to regret their decision. They had had no idea that the plants would be so big, that so many "mountain trash"—as they called the hill people—would descend on their town to work the mills. Now, in addition, had come the strike, which just proved that, in their words, "there warn't no way o' pleasin' some folks." Finally, now "furriners" and "anarchists" were coming in, talking about organizing a trade union, which was the final blow to the people of Elizabethton. Everywhere in the South a trade union was regarded as an invention of the devil, the ultimate weapon devised by the North in its conspiracy to destroy the South.

All this time, I was working busily away at my new job in

Philadelphia, following the developments at Elizabethton only through the meager accounts carried in the newspapers and through the reports we received from our representatives in the field.

I knew well enough who the "furriners" and "anarchists" were who were talking trade union. They were Alfred "Tiny" Hoffman, one of our organizers who had been working in Asheville, North Carolina, and who had immediately driven to Elizabethton (I have seldom met a man 6 foot 2 and 240 pounds who wasn't called "Tiny" by his co-workers) and Edward F. McGrady, legislative agent for the American Federation of Labor (AFL) and general all-round trouble-shooter for AFL president William Green.

On the evening of April 4, 1929, Elizabethton exploded, and the mobs went to work.

One mob broke into McGrady's hotel room, hauled him downstairs and into an automobile, drove him to a lonely spot on a road near Bristol, Virginia, twenty-five miles north, and dumped him out. As he lay by the roadside, one of his captors put a gun against his head, and said: "This is what you get if you come back."

Hoffman got almost exactly the same treatment. A gang broke into his room, blindfolded him and beat him, and drove him over the North Carolina border. He was thrown out of the car, a gun against his head, and a voice told him: "Come back to E-town and get shot, you Jew Yankee bastard."

It was that weekend that the union called me at home and told me to go down and find out what was going on. I found Hoffman in a nursing home, beginning to recover from his beating—and with a self-appointed guard of a half-dozen young girl strikers from Elizabethton, each one of them armed with a pistol she wore in her stocking top.

There wasn't anything I could do for Hoffman except tell the union that he would recover, so I went to Elizabethton to get in touch with those workers who were emerging as the strike leaders. From the start, I got along with them fine. The first thing they warned me about was not to take a room in a local hotel; they were firmly convinced that the hotel manager had been in cahoots with the kidnapers of McGrady and Hoffman, and I'm sure they were right. There was an empty room over a restaurant they frequented, and this they fixed up for me with a cot, a table, and a chair. A volunteer armed guard sat outside my room every night at the top of the stairs, a loaded rifle across his knees.

Why there wasn't even more bloodshed than there was during this strike, I'll never know. The National Guard had been called out, and they patrolled with fixed bayonets and live ammunition in their rifles. The strikers, bred in the mountains and accustomed to handling guns almost from their infancy, also walked the streets with loaded rifles and pistols.

One night one of the strikers I knew only as "Mack," a tough old mountaineer, asked me if I'd like to go for a little ride through the countryside. It had been a long, hard day, and I agreed. I didn't suspect anything even when he drove past the heavily patrolled main gates of the Glanzstoff plant, then stopped alongside the high wire fence a little farther on. Mack dragged a heavy burlap bag out of the back of the car, threw it over the fence, busied himself with it for a few minutes, then ran back to the car, jumped in, and off we drove. A minute later there was a huge explosion behind us. Mack had put ten pounds of dynamite against the fence and lit a fuse. He thought it was a great joke. He just wanted to show me what mountain folk did when they got "riled up."

I began to become seriously worried about this "riled up" feeling. You could almost touch the tension in the air, and I knew that if it exploded into a shooting war, the union would be blamed. I was particularly worried about the strikers who were walking the streets with loaded rifles; I also knew that a mountain man without a gun at hand felt almost naked. Still, I explained my worries to the strike leaders at great length, and after several hours they agreed that they would try to convince their followers that guns would not be carried openly on the streets—provided they knew that the guns would be readily available.

Where did the guns end up?

Under my bed. I am not a gun man at all, but for nights on end I slept with a dozen loaded rifles under my bed.

After I reported back to the union headquarters about Hoffman and the general state of affairs at Elizabethton, I was instructed to stay at Elizabethton and see what I could do about the matter of the court injunction that Bemberg-Glanzstoff had obtained against the strikers. The original injunction had been a temporary one; now the question at issue was whether the court would order it made permanent.

The first problem was to find a lawyer, for though the court had granted the first injunction without a hearing, it had decided that the strikers were entitled to counsel. I had heard of a postgraduate law seminar run in Knoxville by John Randolph Neal, the American Civil Liberties Union lawyer who had assisted Clarence Darrow in the Scopes trial. (Later, I found that almost every outstanding lawyer in Tennessee—Estes Kefauver, later US senator and presidential candidate, to name one—had attended Neal's seminars.)

I managed to get Neal on the telephone. He couldn't take the case (although he did come up for a day to observe it), but he gave me the name of a feisty old criminal lawyer named John Devine who didn't give a damn about corporations, state police, the National Guard, or Chambers of Commerce.

From him—though we were foreordained to lose the case—I began to learn one lesson that was to stand me in good stead later in my lobbying career: How to prepare a case, how to evaluate and organize testimony in advance, how to line up witnesses and brief them on what would happen once they got to the stand.

At this same time, I began to turn out a series of press releases and newspaper stories. The stories ran almost entirely in the labor press—in *Labor,* the one-million-circulation weekly published by the railroad unions, and in the *Federated Press*, the leftist-leaning labor press service that had not yet come under communist control.

In addition, I was able to help some of the labor journalists who had arrived on the scene.

One was Mary Heaton Vorse, a renowned writer on social conditions all through the twenties and thirties, principally for *Harper's* magazine; another was John Moutoux, a Scripps-Howard reporter from Knoxville (who was promptly arrested by the state police when he arrived in Elizabethton and whom I had to bail out of jail); and two whose expenses were paid by Norman Thomas's League for Industrial Democracy (LID): Paul H. Porter, for years the editor of the Kenosha (Wisconsin) *Labor* and later the US mission chief for the Economic Cooperation Administration in Sweden, and John Herling, fresh out of Harvard, who later became perhaps the best-known labor columnist in Washington.

Like so many spontaneous strikes, the one at Elizabethton was doomed from the start. Virtually the whole community stood against the strikers. The mills controlled the town. The police, the courts, the bankers, the politicians, all did Bemberg-Glanzstoff's bidding. Moreover, the mills had money and plenty of it; the union had none, or certainly nowhere near enough to finance strike benefits for a couple of thousand workers for an indefinite period of weeks or months. Norman Thomas tried to help us through the LID, and so did a number of the other liberal organizations, but the money raised amounted to only a drop in the bucket.

I also traded shamelessly on my old Huebsch connection with Sherwood Anderson, and prevailed on him to come to Elizabethton to meet with the strikers. Not that Anderson needed much persuading—people tend to forget how deeply Anderson was dedicated to social reform, how much of his life he gave to social causes. Anderson attended one union meeting we held for the purpose of enrolling new members and later wrote that what struck him about the mood of the meeting was "a kind of religion of brotherhood."

But none of these things achieved anything substantive to help us to win the strike. It became apparent to me that Thomas F. McMahon, then president of UTWU, finally would accept almost any settlement simply to end the strike.

I reached the depths of frustration in my speeches at my daily strike meetings, preaching over and over again about the necessity for unionization, for sticking together, holding out what hopes I could for what could be achieved, all the time knowing in my heart that management had us exactly where they wanted us. After the permanent injunction against the strike was issued by the court, a strike settlement agreement—if it can be called that—was worked out by a young woman named Anna Weinstock, at that time and for years afterward one of the two or three top mediators in the US Conciliation and Mediation Service. The agreement provided basically that the strike would be called off and that the strikers would apply for re-employment; that if a striker was not re-employed, the company would have to give a reason, and if the reason was unsatisfactory, the employee could take the complaint to the mill's personnel manager (!); that management could not discriminate against an employee for union activities, provided the activities were "legitimate"; and finally, that the management would meet with a committee of employees to discuss grievances.

It was a bitter pill, a sellout. But what else could have been done?

It was my responsibility to explain this settlement to the workers. I cannot remember the exact words that I used, but I remember speaking for longer than I should on the necessity for the strike leaders and for those convinced of the justice of the cause to return to work and to build the kind of union solidarity that would be needed in the future.

I like to think that this speech did not fall entirely upon deaf ears. Five years later, the mills in Elizabethton were organized, and they operate under a union contract to this day. That was no solace to me back then, however. The next day, with heavy heart, I took the train back to Philadelphia.

Chapter Five

A FEW MONTHS AFTER I went to work for the Hosiery Workers, I moved my family to the Philadelphia suburb of Flourtown. Flourtown, a village ten miles north of the center of downtown Philadelphia, with a population—when we moved there—of less than two thousand, was located in the heart of a district of magnificent estates belonging to the Wideners, the Stotesburys, and the Carsons. The posh Whitemarsh Valley Hunt Club was situated across a field from our home. The village itself was populated largely by employees—"retainers," they were still called in those days—of the big estates, plus the "village people" themselves, exactly the way rural society was established in England. The main street of Flourtown was called the "Bethlehem Pike," it being the main road north from Philadelphia to Bethlehem, dating back to Revolutionary days. Along the Pike straggled the post office, the fire station, a rambling old inn mostly housing overflow guests from the big houses, a meat market, a candy store, a couple of groceries, a drug store, and so on.

At the end of our road was a Catholic convent, and I still

remember the terrible faux pas made by the mother superior on election day in 1928 when she led all her nuns, in full habit, down the main street to the polling booths to vote for Alfred E. Smith for president. In Republican Flourtown, you do *not* march nuns down the street to vote for a Catholic!

I still remember, too, that every Christmas Day old Mr. Stotesbury (this was before his involvement with Ivar Krueger, the Swedish "match king," had become a matter of public scandal and he had to flee the country) would send his coach-and-four down the main street, liveried footmen blowing their bugles, to deliver his presents to his workers. One old man, I remember, always received a five-pound package of tobacco and was delighted with it.

Our house was a sturdy remodeled old Pennsylvania Dutch farmhouse made of stone, set off on a side street and surrounded by two acres of land.

Behind the house was a large barn, and beyond that an old summer house in which we could accommodate guests. Beyond that was the training track for the horses of the Widener racing stable where, on Saturday afternoons, there would sometimes be training races. Once, I remember, I invited some girls from the office of the Hosiery Workers out on a lovely fall Saturday to watch these impromptu races from a hillside on our place; and the output of work in the office the following week was severely curtailed. All unknowing, we had spent the entire afternoon lolling in clumps of sumac in the full bloom of poison.

Flourtown was a magnificent environment in which to bring up children. Our three grew up quite normally—they thoroughly disapproved of their parents, and they detested each other. The major indictment against me was that I was away from home too much. I remember, in fact, Alison once asking her mother: "Mummy, do you remember when Daddy used to live with us?" The indictment against Kate was that she was far too strict and did not set a table that met their standards. Their idea of a well-balanced meal included meat, preferably hamburger, white bread, and ice cream. The drink, soda pop. Kate's idea was cheese; homemade, mill-ground, whole wheat bread (or pumpernickel); and salad. The drink, milk. Alison's attitude toward her younger siblings was that Arnold was an unspeakable boor and Anne a scheming minx. Arnold's was that Alison was an insufferable prig and Anne a scheming minx. Anne's was that everyone was picking on her because she was the youngest; how she had been born into such an undistinguished middle-class family in the first place was a mystery beyond all understanding.

I believe that all of these judgments later mellowed.

From a parent's point of view, nonetheless, Flourtown was a fine place for children. There was the country, the fields in which to play, places to go swimming, plenty of other children around with whom to play.

The main reason that we had moved to Flourtown, however, was the Carson School for Girls, an educational institution primarily for orphan girls that had been established by Robert Carson, a multimillionaire streetcar magnate. It was directed by Elsa Ueland, who had made her reputation as an educator while assistant superintendent of the Gary, Indiana, public schools, and who was running Carson on the most progressive and idealistic of standards. Miss Ueland had offered Kate a part-time job teaching at the Carson School and said that our girls could attend school there. They did, too, until they were ready for high school.

The Flourtown of that day—indeed, the whole Philadelphia area of that day—had an atmosphere that reminded me somewhat of the atmosphere of my younger years in England. Besides the gentry, there were a great many people deeply involved with social progress, social ideas, the whole cultural ferment of the time. One of the most important to me was Morris Llewellyn Cooke. A mechanical engineer by training, he was the most distinguished protégé of Frederick W. Taylor, the founder of "Scientific Management"—the forerunner of today's "efficiency experts" and "productivity studies."

I first met Cooke at a labor institute at which the president of the Hosiery Workers, Gustave Geiges, read a paper I wrote for him called "Waste in the Full-Fashioned Industry." Ladies' "full-fashioned hosiery" in those days still was made almost entirely of silk. (Bemberg-Glanzstoff represented a rare exception.) Silk was a delicate and expensive fiber, and spoilage was a major expense in the operation of the mills. Geiges's speech argued that if management and labor would cooperate, such spoilage could be diminished. Labor's cooperation would be assured, he said, if management would agree to spend part of its savings on increasing wages and improving working conditions.

Cooke was delighted with the approach. As far as I know, Hosiery was the first union in the United States to take the sophisticated approach of trying to bring labor, technology, and management closer together, and from this time on, because he knew I had written the speech, Cooke and I were fast friends.

At Flourtown, I early became involved in what was in later years to be one of my major preoccupations: protection of the consumer. As part of my public relations duties at Hosiery, I became actively involved in promoting what we then called the "white list"—recommending the products of manufacturers who employed union labor.

The term had been invented by the women who had formed the National Consumers League in 1899 to fight sweatshop conditions and who had first devised the campaign of persuading women to buy only those undergarments that bore a "union label." The founding mother of the league was a magnificent social pioneer, Mrs. Florence Kelley, one of the earliest graduates of Cornell (Cornell was founded in 1868, and she was graduated in 1882), one of the nation's first woman lawyers (Northwestern Law School, 1894), and a crusader for women's and children's protection all her life. Among her close associates were Miss Frances Perkins (later to be secretary of labor under President Franklin Roosevelt), who worked with Mrs. Kelley at Hull House in Chicago, and Mrs. Franklin D. Roosevelt, a staunch supporter of the league throughout her life.

I went to New York (then home of the Consumers League headquarters) to get Mrs. Kelley's approval for league support of a campaign the union was then launching to get women to buy only union-made hosiery. The league had never before entered into a campaign with a union, and its own drive for union-made goods had never extended to hosiery. For my campaign, I had gotten an artist to make a pen-and-ink drawing of a leggy beauty, à la Aubrey Beardsley, standing atop a hill, the wind blowing her skirts above her thighs. It bore the legend "Wear Union-Made Hosiery." The manufacturers and the advertising agencies were finding that pictures of lovely, long-legged beauties could sell anything from stockings to automobiles, so why shouldn't I cash in on the same technique?

Mrs. Kelley was well into her sixties when I first saw her (she died in 1932, at age seventy-three) and already an invalid, lying on a reclining chair in her office and covered with blankets, but her mind was alert and inquiring. She was rather imperious, but we got along quite well. I had been told that I could have only a few minutes with her, but she kept me almost an hour, cross-examining me about the union and about the campaign. Her questions made me fairly sure that she had gone to the trouble of finding out all about me, the union, *and* the campaign before she had ever agreed to receive me. I felt as if I were in the presence of Queen Victoria.

Most important of all, she agreed to support the campaign. The league didn't have much of a mailing list, but it had enormous prestige; that we had its imprimatur was a great feather in our cap. I later joined the board of the league (and still later was chairman) largely out of a sense of gratitude to Mrs. Kelley. It was only as the years passed that I developed a number of rewarding relationships from my work with the league: Mrs. Roosevelt, of course, and Mary Dublin (today Mrs. Leon Keyserling), Frances Perkins, and the league's present executive director, Mrs. Sarah Newman, who probably did more than any other single person to bring the present Truth-in-Lending Act to final passage.

Moving to Philadelphia broadened the horizons of my life in two other ways that I hadn't foreseen when I had agreed to the change. For example, it plunged me deep into the field of workers' education. I had first become convinced of the need for workers' education from my days in England, and it was to remain an important part of my work throughout my life.

Workers' education was very much a stepchild in the Federation in those days. The Federation's Workers' Education Bureau was looked on with some distaste even by Samuel Gompers, under whose presidency it had been established in 1922. I never knew Gompers (who died in 1924) personally, but it was impossible to be even a moderately intelligent American citizen in those days, much less a labor skate, without knowing a good deal *about* Gompers.

He had led the American labor movement onto the path of respectability, principally because of his role in World War I when he had organized and headed the War Committee on Labor and had become a leading member of the Advisory Commission to the Council of National Defense. In these twin roles he had personified labor as loyal to the government, denying its image as a collection of ravaging anarchists which had grown out of the newspaper accounts of violence by the Molly Maguires and the Wobblies.

One major reason that Gompers had been able to change the public feeling about labor to such an extent was that his war activities had given him a public aura of conservatism. Born in London, he had been brought to this country by his parents when he was thirteen (in 1863) and was put to work as an apprentice cigar maker; he became president of his local union and, in 1881, a founder of the Federation of Organized Trades and Labor Unions, which later became the AFL. Gompers was very much the heir of the tradition of a labor union as a trade union—a banding together of skilled craftsmen to improve their economic lot in the world. In addition, he had before him the object lesson of what had happened to the Knights of Labor.

The Knights of Labor, in its day, had been the most progressive labor organization in the world. Founded as a secret organization by a group of Philadelphia tailors in 1869, it gradually expanded—and slowly abandoned its secrecy—

until in 1881 it formally incorporated as a nationwide industrial union. It took women, blacks, and even employers into its ranks; its membership mushroomed across the country (attaining a high of 700,000); it won strikes against the Wabash and Union Pacific Railroads. It believed in workers' education with a vengeance and strove to achieve through education its goals of equal pay for equal work, abolition of private banks, establishment of cooperatives, the eight-hour day, and so on. Unfortunately, a variety of causes led to its downfall: an increasingly autocratic leadership, expensive strikes that it lost, and most important of all—something that was to plague the AFL itself so much later on—internal jurisdictional disputes.

Gompers, who was in the vanguard of the fight against the Knights of Labor in establishing the AFL, drew one lesson from its demise: There was no place in a labor organization for "crusades" for social objectives. A labor union should confine itself to attending to the welfare of its dues-paying members.

This being the philosophy of Gompers and of his equally conservative successor, the old secretary-treasurer of the United Mine Workers, William Green, it is hardly surprising that workers' education was very much a fifth-rate issue in the AFL when I went to Philadelphia.

If I needed substantive proof of this, it lay in the fact that workers' education came under the purview of AFL vice-president Matthew Woll. A tough, taciturn, unimaginative, red-faced cigar smoker, Woll was basically dedicated to the principle that the first function of a union leader was to keep himself in power so that he could continue to enjoy his fine salary and fat expense account. He regarded the workers' education program as a subversive exercise that would result only in teaching workers to ask questions that he regarded as impertinent.

Even my old friend Jim Maurer, who was himself an officer of the Workers' Education Bureau—by which I mean that his name was on the letterhead of the official stationery—regarded the program as a joke.

"Teaching workers about the democratic process and the role of labor in the economy, for Christ's sake," Maurer told me. "Why not just teach 'em to to read and write and let it go at that?"

What Woll didn't want was workers learning enough to demand democracy in local meetings, to demand to be allowed to vote on issues, and to nominate candidates for local union offices instead of just passing on the program the hierarchy presented to them.

In view of all this official hostility, it was surprising that the federation had an educational program for workers at all. But there were other factors in its favor. In the first place, the federation was not a completely monolithic organization. On the one hand, it had its hidebound craft unions—the carpenters, the plumbers, Matt Woll's photoengravers—but on the other hand, it also had David Dubinsky's International Ladies Garment Workers Union (ILGWU) and, of course, the Hosiery Workers. Both these latter unions had been in the forefront of establishing workers' education programs; indeed, the ILGWU, because its membership included so many European Jews starved for education of any sort and bent on assimilating American culture, had begun the first really organized union educational program in the nation.

In addition to these pressures within the federation, the whole field of workers' education, following in the British tradition, had gotten an entirely new impetus in the 1920s. Workers' education was an offspring of the whole concept of adult education, the tradition of night classes and other systems of extra-hierarchical learning, the results of the activities of the Quakers and other church groups, of the Young Women's Christian Association (YWCA), of various colleges and universities, community groups, and so on.

Because of the amalgam of all these factors, the AFL finally did set up its workers' education program. What I really didn't understand when I entered the program was how the sheer dead weight of the AFL top executives who didn't believe in or care about workers' education would make the program effective.

When I first became involved in the program, a man named Spencer Miller was executive director. In some ways I had great respect for him, and in others, pity. A well-educated man with the best of instincts, he enjoyed a substantial reputation in social work. But he possessed almost no grasp of the basic conflict that existed between employers and workers—class conflict, if you will—and he was not at all at ease in talking with, or dealing with, groups of workers. Not even with craft-union workers, who are, to this day, entirely middle class in their outlook.

One of the few bright spots in my early days was meeting E. J. Lever, a skilled machinist, a socialist, and a man as dedicated to workers' education as I was. In those days the Socialist Party and the Jewish Labor Committee had a joint headquarters in South Philadelphia, to a large extent a gathering place for the non-English-speaking people in the trade-union movement, and Lever, Jewish as well as socialist, was very much in evidence around the headquarters. A bustler of a man, and a natural-born teacher, he had a pivotal role in starting an educational institute at this headquarters called the Labor Institute; from him I got many insights into what role workers' education should play, the methods and techniques it should employ.

Lever left Philadelphia only a short while after I had begun to know him well, to become general manager of Brookwood, in New York state, the only residential labor college that existed in the country at that time (and one of the few in the world).

I persuaded a number of young men in Hosiery to attend lectures and forums at the Labor Institute. It took a certain amount of persuasion. The measure of distance was not great, but there was the usual measure of human inertia. North Philadelphia was where, by and large, working people lived, and it was the natural habitat of these young Hosiery Workers. Getting them to make the trip to the Labor Institute in South Philadelphia, after a full day's work, became more and more of a chore.

After a while, I decided that the effort involved in setting up these trips was simply more than it was worth. I decided to devote my labor-education work to giving classes myself at the headquarters of the Hosiery Workers. I began with a course on the history of the labor movement in the United States, based on the first volumes of John R. Commons's *History of Labor in the United States.*

It took me only a short time to realize that this pedantic method of teaching was not achieving those goals that I wanted to realize in my course. I wanted to teach my students two basic things: the role that labor had played and could play in the American economy, and the way that a democracy could and should function, not only on the political scene but also within labor unions themselves. Teaching the history of the American labor movement could provide a useful background for this, but it was only a background.

At the Hosiery Workers, I felt, the workers—so many of them immigrants—were truly excited by the concept of democracy, by debates and reports and elections. Here they could actually see a free society in operation, and from then on I devoted as much of my lecture time as possible to explaining how this system worked. I took the same approach when, at Lever's invitation, I lectured at Brookwood Labor College.

Brookwood's weakness was that it was ahead of its time. The American labor movement wasn't ready for it. Some of the old-time AFL leaders were appalled at the thought of a labor college teaching courses advocating that democratic methods be introduced into the system of electing trade-union officials. In fact, old Matt Woll, in 1929, put Brookwood on a list of "radical" institutions maintained by the AFL itself. The way Brookwood did teach was its proper function, in my opinion; it was a great pity that it was allowed to die.

Brookwood closed, finally, not because of Woll's enmity nor because of the opposition, but simply because it could not get enough support in or out of the trade-union movement. When it closed, I—along with a lot of other people—felt the kind of futility known only to those who have fought the good fight and lost, not because of the strength of the opposition but simply out of general apathy. We at Hosiery felt the loss more deeply than most because we had been helping support Brookwood financially in the face of considerable rancor at AFL headquarters.

Another residential labor school with which I was associated ran for ten years, from 1929 to 1939. This was the Hudson Shore Labor School, a summer school held on the estate of Hilda Smith just above Poughkeepsie, New York. Miss Smith and her sister were the last two remaining members of a well-to-do New York family.

Miss Smith, a sparkling white-haired lady when I first knew her, concealed enormous drive and devotion to social betterment under such a prim and ladylike exterior that she was known universally to her colleagues as "Jane" (from "plain Jane," I suppose). Formerly dean of Bryn Mawr College, she was devoted to the principle that education should not be restricted to the upper classes. For years, during the late twenties and early thirties, she had conducted the Bryn Mawr Summer School for Women Workers in Industry on the Bryn Mawr campus outside Philadelphia. (The summer school itself had been founded in 1921 by Dr. Susan Kingsbury, head of the Department of Sociology at Bryn Mawr, at the suggestion of the ILGWU in New York, to hold courses for its workers during the summer.)

It was there that I had first gotten to know Hilda Smith, for I had been a lecturer at the school, and the way that came about is another example of the coming together of the various traditions of workers' education mentioned earlier.

One of the important organizations in this field was the YWCA. In those days—at least in eastern Pennsylvania, with which I was most familiar—the young girls who came to work in the mills were basically a group of shy, timid, frightened creatures. Many of them had come straight to the mills to get away from the drudgery of farm work or the grinding poverty of rural life. After work in the mill had ended for the day, one of the few places these girls could visit for a few hours of relaxation was the local "Y." The Y realized this and set up all sorts of programs for them: lectures, dances, courses. The program became so large, in fact, that the Y set up an entire industrial department.

My leftist friends in the labor movement at that time were fond of attacking the Y industrial programs as "escapism" and "company unionism," but I was more pragmatic. A good many of these girls worked in hosiery mills, and I soon saw that the Y had an appeal for them that no labor union could hope to match. The Y was, to some degree, a home away from home for them. (My leftist friends to the contrary, the Y branch in northeast Philadelphia, near the Hosiery headquarters, became so important in labor-industry relations that it was recognized as the headquarters for the arbitration machinery of the industry in that area, and the Y building was regularly used for union-management conferences and arbitration hearings.) I made it my business, therefore, to get myself invited to lectures, conferences, and other affairs run by the Y; after a while I became a fairly popular speaker.

It was also through these Y classes that many of the girls heard of the Bryn Mawr summer school and attended classes. The Y did make a meaningful contribution to the cause of organized labor in the 1920s, especially important at a time when the general mood of the country was basically antilabor.

Besides running the Bryn Mawr summer school, Hilda Smith had almost singlehandedly raised the money to keep it alive through ten-odd years, until the Depression put an end to it, as it did to almost all ventures of this sort. At that point, using her family estate as the administration-library-classroom headquarters for Hudson Shore, scraping money together from whatever sources she could (mostly small donations from the Ivy League women's colleges—Bryn Mawr, Vassar, Wellesley, and Mount Holyoke, mainly—and from unions with educational departments) and holding expenses to the bone (all I or any of the other lecturers got was travel money and room and board), Hilda was able to keep Hudson Shore school going for a few years.

For me, there were some non-monetary compensations for teaching there. It got me away from the day-to-day drudgery of the union; it provided me with a set of students who were deeply interested in what I had to teach; and it gave me the chance to enjoy the lovely summer weather of the Hudson river countryside. Eventually, however, the problem of finding money to keep Hudson Shore going became impossible, and Hilda had to give it up. By that time the Works Progress Administration (WPA) was in operation, and she was named director of its Workers' Education Project (WEP).

A great many jokes were made at the time about the WPA and its "leaf rakers," and it came in for some bitter criticism—some of it deserved—but I think it was one of the great programs of the New Deal; one of its great accomplishments, with which I was connected, was the WEP.

In my opinion it was the most solid and exciting adult-education effort of any magnitude ever attempted in this country. It was truly experimental; it imparted needed and useful information; and it gave its participants a real sense of purpose. In fact, I feel that if the American labor movement ever aspires to become something more important in the fabric of the country than just an instrument for getting ever higher wages for its members and upgrading substandard workers into better jobs, it will have to return to the concept of the old WEP.

One incident that occurred in the early days of the WEP forever settled in my mind the question that was being speculated about in the newspaper columns in those days: whether Mrs. Roosevelt had influence with the president in the administration of government.

The head of the so-called "white collar" projects in the WPA then, which included the WEP, was a tough-talking, forceful administrator named John Carmody, who had been told by his legal counsel that a certain project proposed in Workers' Education was absolutely not authorized by the terms of the congressional act creating the WPA. Carmody was so convinced of the necessity of this project that he arranged a meeting with Mrs. Roosevelt, some of the WPA people, and myself. The meeting was to be held in the White House. Carmody and I happened to arrive at the White House simultaneously, and we walked into the meeting room together.

Everyone else had already gathered, except for Mrs. Roosevelt, which was unusual for her. Despite a schedule that would baffle Clotho, she was almost always on time. There was nothing for the rest of us to do except to make polite and meaningless conversation until she arrived.

Finally Mrs. Roosevelt came bustling into the room with that radiant smile of hers and went straight to Carmody.

"John," she said, "I've just been talking to Franklin, and he has the solution for your whole problem. He said, why don't you just fire your present man and get yourself a new chief counsel?"

For a moment there was complete silence, then everyone broke into roars of laughter.

"By God, I will!" said Carmody. And the meeting broke up.

I had one final experience with workers' education, and one that I think was perhaps the most satisfying of all. It came during the glowing, optimistic days of the Marshall Plan, shortly after the end of World War II, when newly independent nations were beginning to come into existence and when the US government was officially committed to a policy of assisting free trade unions around the world. A sort of fraternal workers' internationale, so to speak.

I think that the most important phase of the government program was that which brought, over a period of twelve years, some twenty thousand workers to visit the United States to see for themselves how our system worked. Most of these workers were chosen at the factory level, and the only requirement made by this country was that after they returned to their homes, they had to write a report—favorable, unfavorable, or middle-of-the-road—on what they had seen and learned. There had to be two copies of the report at a minimum, one for the US Department of State and one for the local sponsoring organization that had recommended the candidate. It was surprising how many of the reports were unfavorable from workers whom you would have expected to be favorable—those from British automobile factories, for example, who thought American plants too automated, with no time out for tea—and so many favorable from those whom you would expect to be unfavorable—such as oil workers from India, who thought America so much more efficient.

There were two problems in the program. One was the endemic lack of funds; the other was the difficulty of placing foreign workers in the homes of American workers. This had been a basic dream of the original planners, but they had underestimated the difficulties of the language problems involved and the natural tendency of people from a foreign country to stay together. In other words, if six steel workers from France came to this country, it was almost impossible to find French-speaking American steel workers, and the Frenchmen themselves preferred to stay together rather than go off into separate American homes. This was all perfectly understandable, but it did effectively defeat the purpose of having the foreign workers see how the American worker actually lived.

My own role in the program consisted of being an adviser to the State Department and the Labor Department on the arrangements for the visitors—where they should go, what they should visit, where they should stay—and a lecturer and what was called, in that terrible government jargon, a "briefing" and "debriefing" officer. That meant that when the teams arrived in this country, I gave a series of introductory lectures about how the American system worked, American customs, the American trade-union organization, down to the American monetary system of pennies, nickels, and dimes. This was the "briefing." When they returned to Washington after their stay in what was called "the interior," there were the "debriefing" sessions at which I and the other lecturers were supposed to explain to them what they had seen and to answer the almost endless questions that had arisen in their minds during their visits.

Most of these sessions took place on the beautiful and picturesque campus of St. John's College in Annapolis. The government paid only a token fee to its lecturers, but I was more than delighted to take part in the program, partly from the satisfaction I had in trying to explain the American political and trade-union systems to those from abroad (especially the visitors from Africa and Asia) and partly from listening to their explanations of how totally alien our philosophy was from theirs.

Strangely enough, despite all the highly philosophical discussions I had with these foreign visitors, it is a purely human and physical problem that I remember most clearly. In many cases, the allowance paid to each of these overseas workers, especially those from Africa, meager as it was, represented quite a good deal of money to them, and their instinct was to save as much of it as possible to send back to their families. I remember going to Chicago in the winter of 1957 to speak at a meeting of the regional Textile Workers Union of America (TWUA) and on the way to the airport, William J. Tullar, the Midwest TWUA director, mentioned to me that he was faced with a problem with eight young African workers who had been placed there. They were so anxious to save money, Tullar told me, that they saw no point at all in buying overcoats to help them get through the Chicago winter. (After all, American winter overcoats would be of small use back in Africa.) The result, Tullar said, was that he was afraid they were all going to freeze to death. I believed him. It has been my experience that, even with an overcoat, it is possible to freeze to death in Chicago in the winter, and, moreover, they were getting very little out of the trip. The minute they had finished their day's stint in the textile factory where they had been placed to work and to observe, they simply went back to the quarters that had been found for them in a small hotel and huddled around the radiator. They wouldn't venture out to attend meetings, walk the streets, or even visit the host homes to which they had been invited.

Tullar himself was eventually able to solve that particular problem by dipping into union funds (I was careful never to ask him how) to buy some serviceable winter clothing for his protégés. But I realized that this problem was not confined to Chicago, and when I returned to Washington, I got in touch with an old friend of mine from the Hosiery days in Philadelphia, Alexander Kellenbenz, who was in charge of the workers exchange program for the Economic Cooperation

Administration, the official title of the Marshall Plan. Alex arranged for me to explain the problem to a few of the administrators of ECA, and I was able to convince them of the necessity for establishing a small contingency fund that would cover matters like the purchase of winter overcoats for Africans in Chicago.

In fact, the subject of proper clothing, as a result of this episode, became part of the regular briefing procedure for all incoming trade-union exchangees, and some Washington clothing store owners, eager to do their part to help the program, set up a system whereby they would provide extra needed clothing for our visitors and then, when they were about to leave, take it back at what amounted to nothing more than a modest rental fee and have the clothing rehabilitated for the next visitors.

In a way, you might say that my career in workers' education ended with a small flier into the used-clothing business.

Chapter Six

MANY OF THE events in which I took part at that time turned out to be historic, although, understandably, I did not realize it then. One of those events occurred in August of 1933, when a long, bitter, and often bloody hosiery strike that had encompassed all of the mills in Berks county, Pennsylvania, the second-largest hosiery center in the nation after Philadelphia, was brought to an end by a formula devised by the hastily conceived and newly created National Labor Board (NLB) in Washington. (Berks county, just northwest of Philadelphia, was the nation's second largest hosiery center after Philadelphia.)

The Hosiery Workers had made several attempts to organize the Berks County workers, without much success. Early in 1933, we had decided to try again. The passage of the National Recovery Act with its famous Section 7-A—that extremely ambiguous assertion of the rights of workers to organize—struck a totally unexpected spark among the unorganized workers of the Depression days. They suddenly decided that perhaps now it would be safe to join a union without the danger of being fired.

We in Hosiery were not slow to interpret Section 7-A's guarantee of the rights of workers to join unions "of their own choosing" as in fact a call by the federal government to non-union workers to join up. So we went back to Reading, the county seat of Berks County, with high hopes for the success of our new drive.

Practically the first thing we did was to set up a "tent city" on the Socialist Party's picnic grounds a few miles west of Reading. The tents were old army command-post surplus, measuring about twenty by thirty feet each. We made one the temporary headquarters for the organizing drive, where we kept posters and leaflets and other materials and had our desks and a place to enroll anyone who wanted to drop by and sign up. (We had a permanent headquarters in a Reading office building, but it was far too small.) The other tents held a combined kitchen-mess hall and supplies and provided sleeping quarters for union officials—meaning Emil Rieve, head of the Hosiery Workers in Philadelphia, and me—and about a hundred unemployed union hosiery workers from Philadelphia, North Jersey, and other nearby places. These were our organizers. Rieve and I had been sharing a room in a Reading hotel, but it was miserably rainy weather, and we decided it wouldn't look right for the brass to be occupying a nice, warm hotel room while everyone else was cold, wet, and miserable.

Our organizers were mostly men who had originally come from the Reading area (a small detachment of them headed by a man named Harry Haines were veterans of World War I who actually ran the camp, doing the cooking, policing up, and so on), which was basically a Pennsylvania Dutch district in which most of the older workers spoke an American variant of a south German dialect called Schwabish.

I had cause to remember vividly that, years before, Jim Maurer (who himself spoke Schwabish) had told me that the Reading area was widely regarded by theater people as one of the toughest sections in the country in which to perform.

Comedians never got a laugh, jugglers never received applause. That's about what happened to our organizing drive. We got no applause.

It looked as though we were doomed to fail. Our organizers had spent all their days and most of their evenings going from house to house to talk to unorganized workers and their families. It had taken the organizing staff and me six or seven years to build up the lists of the unorganized workers, but it seemed that it would all go for naught. The organizing drive remained stalled. Despite the fact that most of the mills were closed because of the Depression, the workers, most of whom were out of jobs, still did not sign up in any meaningful numbers. Eventually, after six weeks, we gave up on the drive, struck our tents, and left. We had simply underestimated the fear-inspired inertia that kept these people in misery.

It was several weeks before a different reaction to our drive began to make itself felt. As Maurer used to say about the theater people, the general reaction of the Pennsylvania Dutch to anything was, "Well, let's go down and hear what the fellow has to say." Then, after they had sat on their hands and the show had long since left, one of them would say to another, "You remember that show was here a while back? Wasn't too bad at all."

A few weeks after we had given up, the slow-moving workers began to think that maybe our show wasn't too bad, either. They began to drift into regular union headquarters in Reading, individually or two or three at a time, laconic and somewhat shamefaced, to sign up.

There was one man in particular whom I recall, a knitter who had lived on the same street with the Edelmans in Reading. For several years, when I would meet him on the sidewalk, he would never say more than "good morning" or "good evening." But after he had signed up with the union, he stopped me on the street and insisted on shaking hands.

"Today I can meet you right, Mr. Edelman," he said.

Once the first workers joined the union, they seemed to act as a catalyst on the others. We were simply flooded with applicants. I had returned to Philadelphia after we had closed "tent city," and the first knowledge I had of the situation was when our Reading office telephoned to say that it didn't have sufficient help to sign up so many workers—and it was running out of application forms. It was the first and only time that ever happened to me in my entire career in labor. I packed an extra suitcase and moved back to the hotel at Reading for the duration.

Rieve and I had agreed that we simply *had* to call a strike. The employers had made it crystal clear to us that they were not going to recognize any union as spokesman for the workers, that they were not going to negotiate with us under any circumstances, period. The employers had likewise warned their own workers.

Under those circumstances, the influx of workers who signed with us seemed to qualify as no less than a minor miracle. A union was a totally unknown quantity as far as these workers were concerned, and it was a mark of their desperation that they turned to us. For all they knew, they were committing economic suicide. But we were their last hope. With our new membership, we found that the mill owners would not negotiate with us, and we called a strike.

Within a period of a few days, ten thousand workers were on strike throughout the county, and the violence had begun. There were fights and mass arrests at the picket lines; cars were overturned and set afire; gangs of men in cars drove the streets at night firing shotgun blasts at the homes of the strike leaders. I was in the union headquarters one night when two shotgun blasts tore through the roof. I went to Harrisburg the next day and saw my old boss and friend, Governor Pinchot, and explained the situation to him. He ordered out the state police on twenty-four-hour patrols around the Reading area.

I was practically working a twenty-four-hour shift myself. First, I was the union's press representative, which meant dealing with the two daily papers in Reading, the morning *Times* and the evening *Eagle,* plus the local weekly labor paper (run by the socialists) and the handful of out-of-town newspaper and radio men who showed up. I was also editor of the union's own semimonthly paper, the *Hosiery Worker*, and had to write for that. In addition to those duties, I was director of the organizing drive and of the strike itself, which meant speaking at two or three meetings a day, some of them a twenty-five-mile drive from Reading. Additionally, I was chief lobbyist for the union, telephoning every day to Governor Pinchot's office in Harrisburg and to Washington.

In Washington, one of my chief contacts was Sidney Hillman, president of the Amalgamated Clothing Workers Union, who had been called to Washington by President Roosevelt to become labor adviser to the National Recovery Administration (NRA). I was under orders from Rieve to call Hillman every day; I would have, anyway, for I was beginning to know Hillman well myself.

Hillman was a Lithuanian Jew who had come to this country when he was twenty. He was a short, smooth, dark man of many gifts, enormous energy, and great intelligence. He had been a socialist in his youth, and I think that my own European background and my own socialist upbringing drew us together. I had first become acquainted with him a few years earlier when the Amalgamated had begun to try to organize the ever increasing number of clothing manufacturers who were moving their plants from Manhattan to New Jersey and Pennsylvania to escape the union's jurisdiction. The union's organizers were effective in New York, organizing Jewish immigrants, but they were almost a total loss trying to organize native-born rural factory workers, and I was able to be of some help to the union.

Roosevelt came under a good deal of criticism because of his close relationship with Hillman (the phrase "clear it with Sidney" became a sort of rallying cry for Roosevelt's enemies), and, strangely, Hillman was criticized by some labor people for *his* relationship with Roosevelt. Hillman's critics argued that this hurt his effectiveness as a labor leader. I think that this latter criticism has led to Hillman's contributions, to labor and to the country, being much underrated. People now tend to overlook Hillman's consummate skill as a negotiator—but

John L. Lewis recognized it well enough to request that Hillman be one of the chief negotiators for the first contracts for the auto workers, for the rubber workers, and for a number of other unions. And people now forget Hillman's unique contribution—working with Roosevelt—in building an industrial democracy in this country. The overwhelming importance of that became apparent only a few years later in the role that this industrial democracy played in helping win World War II.

Nevertheless, Hillman was of great help to me in the Reading strike with his advice on how to conduct the strike itself and how to deal with the state and federal mediators who had moved in on the scene.

I had no trouble in dealing with Governor Pinchot's office, of course, but trying to get the ear of Secretary of Labor Frances Perkins was quite a different matter. It was understandable because she and her staff were working day and night, but that didn't alleviate my problem. I did, however, have an entrée to Miss Perkins's office. I knew an ex-labor journalist named Heber Blankenhorn who, sometime in 1933, had been taken onto the staff of Sen. Robert F. Wagner of New York. Through Blankenhorn, I was able to get my case for the Reading workers to the senator, and through the senator to Miss Perkins. It was from Blankenhorn, as a matter of fact, that I first heard that the NLB was being set up in Washington.

The Reading strike was, as I said, brought to an end by a formula, later to become known as "the Reading formula," set up by the NLB. The board itself was created to deal with labor disputes arising from decisions of the NRA headed by that truculent and tough-minded old army general, Hugh S. Johnson. Section 7-A of the National Industrial Recovery Act called for collective bargaining and mutual agreements between employers and workers, but trying to get them established was a very different matter, and that was what the NLB was set up to do.

The NLB had as its first chairman a "public" member, Senator Wagner; three labor members—AFL president William Green, United Mine Workers (UMW) president John L. Lewis, and Dr. Leo Wollman, a brilliant Columbia University professor and alter ego to Sidney Hillman; and three industry members—Louis Kirstein, president of Filene Brothers department stores in Boston; Standard Oil Company of New Jersey president Walter C. Teagle; and Gerard Swope, president of General Electric. To Swope, a liberal industrialist and longtime power in Democratic politics, should go the greatest share of the credit for working out the final shape of the Reading formula.

The formula, as it finally emerged, had four main points: (1) We (the union) were to call an end to the strike; (2) striking employees were to be rehired without discrimination against them because of their strike activities; (3) the board itself would conduct elections in which the workers would vote on who was to represent them, and the employers would negotiate with those elected to establish a collective bargaining contract; and (4) unresolved issues would be submitted to the board for decision. The crux of the agreement was the government-supervised secret election, which was the suggestion of Gerard Swope.

Shortly after I had heard from Blankenhorn that the board was being set up, I received a telephone call from the man who had been named its executive secretary, William M. Leiserson, inviting me, Rieve, and other union representatives to a special meeting of the board to be held in Washington on the afternoon of August 10.

Rieve, as it happened, was already in Washington, attending meetings of an ad hoc committee in the NRA that was setting up the administration of the Hosiery code.

I arranged for two carloads of Reading strike leaders. They were headed by the Reading local president, Henry I. Adams, all dolled up in his bowler and his best black suit, which he generally reserved for funerals and weddings. Our two-car cavalcade wound its way along the narrow roads of the back woods of the beautiful Pennsylvania Dutch countryside through the lovely summer morning, crossed the bridge over the Delaware, through the maze of streets of slowly awakening Baltimore, and reached Washington about ten in the morning. We met Rieve at the Hotel Continental, opposite the magnificent two-hundred-acre Union Station Plaza. Rieve gave us a short briefing over coffee about what was happening (as far as the Hosiery Workers were concerned) in Washington. I then led our little delegation on foot to the House side of the Capitol to sit in for a while on the Hosiery code hearing. We went for lunch in the cafeteria of the then brand-new Department of Commerce building downtown, then to the Labor Board hearing, which was being held in the building and which began, naturally, late.

It was at this meeting that Swope proposed the idea of secret elections to determine a bargaining representative. It was the "secret election" clause that moved the employers to agree, for the owners of the unorganized mills were convinced that their workers did not want to be represented by a union and, if given the choice, would vote it down.

It was well into the evening before the meeting came to its end on this accord, and Wollman called in the three or four reporters who had been waiting in the Commerce Building press room to announce it. After everyone had left the press room, I sat down at a desk and typed out a release in Rieve's name and called the wire services and the Reading papers and read it to them.

It was after midnight before I got back to the Hotel Continental, where the Reading delegation was sitting around talking to Rieve. I showed Rieve the press release, and then all of us from Reading piled into the cars and started the drive back.

When we got back to Reading around daylight practically everyone started for our forty-odd picket lines to explain what had happened. I washed, shaved, and had a quick breakfast at my hotel; by eight I was holding a press conference to explain in detail to the local reporters what had happened.

Then I got on the phone back to Washington, to Leiserson and Blankenhorn. It had dawned on me that I had no more than the vaguest idea of precisely how to go about setting up the secret-ballot elections that we were to hold—even, for example, how to make up the ballots, where and when (including the hours) to establish the polling booths, how to ensure secrecy, and innumerable other details.

This was the first such election in American labor history, and it turned out that neither Leiserson nor Blankenhorn knew much more than I. They did tell me, however, that the NLB had gotten the services of Fred M. Wilcox, a retired member of the Industrial Relations Commission of Wisconsin and close friend of Sen. Robert LaFollette, to help out.

For all of Wilcox's qualifications, his experience hadn't given him insights into the task he was facing. The really major contribution to the election came from the then-retiring mayor of Reading, a magnificent old socialist named J. Henry Stump, one of the most clear-headed and persuasive men I have ever met.

My own experience stood us in good stead at the very first meeting that Wilcox set up between the employers and the union to establish the procedures for the election. The employers asked that the list of qualified voters be established by the union's turning over its membership lists to be checked against the payroll records of the companies. Of course, for years the companies had been employing a notorious labor spy agency called the Railway Audit and Inspection Company (later exposed in hearings conducted by the younger Robert LaFollette when he followed in his father's footsteps to the US Senate) for the very purpose of getting the lists of dues-paying union members.

We knew that so well, and the employers knew that we knew it so well, that I'm sure that the proposal was put forward more as a ploy than anything else. To my horror, Wilcox took it seriously. He and I fortunately had gotten along rather well when we had first been introduced, and after that first joint meeting, I was able to explain to him some of the basic facts of life about labor-employer relations and persuade him to reject the employers' suggestion.

In the next couple of meetings, we did not take any substantive step forward as to how we were going to establish the voting list. At this point I had a small inspiration. I knew that, besides all his intellectual qualities, Stump had had years of practical experience in the rough-and-tumble Reading city politics, and I arranged a secret meeting between him and Wilcox.

At the meeting Stump made a point so lucid and so simple that it has been used ever since by the National Labor Relations Board as the basis for making up the list of eligible voters in representation elections.

"Since the point of these lists," he told Wilcox, "is to establish who are and who are not bona-fide employees of the mills involved and to frustrate the possibility of either side bringing in a lot of non-employees, or temporary employees, why not just use the payroll lists of the companies? They're not secret."

This practice is so universal today that it may not seem like much of an inspiration. But, when seeking just procedures at the beginning of any new social process, nothing is as simple as it seems afterward. It is as though we had been trying to grope our way out of a swamp at night and someone said: "Follow that line of trees there." Everyone who comes to the edge of the swamp afterward asks, "That's so simple and obvious, why couldn't they have seen it back then?" They weren't in the swamp that night, is why.

Stump did more than just make the suggestion to Wilcox. He sat there and dictated to Wilcox an outline of precisely how the election machinery should be set up and the way in which the election should be carried out; he then told Wilcox that he would lend him, as the NLB's official representative, the city's official ballot boxes and other election equipment and arrange to have it transported to designated polling places, at the proper time, in the city of Reading's municipal trucks.

When Wilcox presented this comprehensive program at the next session with the employers, it was accepted almost without question. With Stump's help, the polling places were determined, all in public buildings—schools and courts—as close to the factories as possible. With the company payroll lists now in his possession, Wilcox sent a letter, signed by him for the NLB, to each employee. Stump got the Berks County judges to agree to donate their time to settle, on the spot, any disputes that might arise over the conduct of the election. Both sides submitted their lists of observers to watch the polls, just as is done in ordinary political elections, with Wilcox over them all as the impartial supervising observer.

The polling places were open on three successive days, a Monday, Tuesday, and Wednesday, and by 8:00 P.M. on Wednesday the last of the ballot boxes had been delivered to Wilcox at the hotel, and the counting began. Within an hour the way the voting was going was apparent. The workers were voting for union representation by more than ten to one.

Elections were held for the employees of forty-five mills in Reading and the surrounding area, and a total of about fourteen thousand workers voted. We won the right to negotiate for the workers in thirty-seven of the mills where we got 13,362 votes; in the other eight mills, with 720 votes, non-union representatives, most of them friendly to management, were chosen.

Naturally, immediately after the election, when we held our first meeting with the owners, thirty-six of the thirty-seven employers present refused to sign a written collective-bargaining agreement, and we had to go back to the NLB in Washington for help.

Late in September, the board ruled that the action of the employers was in defiance of the agreement they had signed to hold the elections, and the employers finally gave in.

Looking back now and recognizing its significance, I suppose that when the election was won, I should have been in ecstasy. But I wasn't. I was delighted, pleased—all the rest. But I didn't really comprehend for a long time afterward that this was the first such election that had ever been held. Today, histories of the thirties refer almost casually to the "Reading formula" and the "Reading election."

All I realized was that we had won the election and that I was in a small hotel in Reading, Pennsylvania, by now exhausted. Even so, I could not just pack my bag and go home to my long-suffering wife and children in triumph, because of all the odds and ends that I still had to take care of.

During the weeks of the hosiery strike, workers in other

industries began to take a leaf out of our book and walk out of their own plants. But the AFL was so hierarchical then, so accustomed to dealing only with situations with which it was familiar, that it was impossible to get the international headquarters of some of these unions to take any organizing action at all.

When we began to get word of these walkouts, Rieve told me that I "ought to keep an eye on them," but I was already working anywhere from fifteen to twenty hours a day. There was a strike in a pretzel factory, of all places, a dress factory, a hat factory, a cotton textile mill, a shoe factory, a leather plant, and a half-dozen other places that I've forgotten.

All I could do to "keep an eye on them" was telephone for help. The only places where I made any progress was with the dress factory where Fred Wilcox, out of the goodness of his heart and as a favor to me, agreed to mediate the dispute, and I was able to get the ILGWU to assume union duties.

I was finally able to leave Reading, four days after the election had been held, the results blazoned in the newspapers, my odds and ends cleaned up.

Chapter Seven

My official title in later days, when I moved to Washington, was "legislative agent." Much as it may sound so, this was not a euphemism on my part for "lobbyist." My first aim was to help frame legislation that would eliminate legal obstacles to a union's building an organization that could assure its members a fair deal at the bargaining table.

The main problem in achieving this aim that I at first encountered was ignorance—not just my own, but everyone else's. In those days, for example, very few universities gave courses in what is now called industrial relations. The labor movement itself had no resources to provide even guidelines as to how to accomplish what I had set out to do. So much of what I did was "by guess and by God."

I had gotten my first experience in the field of legislation in the late 1920s in Pennsylvania and New Jersey where we in Hosiery were trying to move against the so-called "labor spy." Even now when you mention "labor spy" to men in labor, you can almost see their minds harking to the dim and distant past before they say, "Oh, yes, I remember when . . ."

But to us in Hosiery, the labor spy was a very real menace. The technique of the employer was generally very simple. An ostensibly bona-fide worker would be hired and accepted by fellow workers. But his actual role would be to report back to the employer the names of the union members and of the active union supporters among the workers, what the union was doing in the plant in terms of collecting grievances, seeking new members, and so on.

It was an excellent technique, for a generally unrecognized reason.

America as a nation had never had what England knew as "a working class." In England, an average knitter in a mill thought of himself as a member of the "working class" and knew that the most effective way to improve his lot was to belong to the union and to support it in all of its dealings with "the owners."

In America, workers thought of themselves not so much as members of the "working class" but as yet-unrecognized members of the middle class. The American worker, therefore, as compared to the English one, was caught in a cleft stick. He not only felt equal to any man (which made him feel that he did not need the union) but also knew that he might be fired if he did join the union.

The labor spy added a third element. If a worker is disdainful of the union and frightened of joining it, he needs only to suspect that a fellow worker is a spy to make him even more wary.

Labor spying then was so much an accepted practice in the business community that the major suppliers of spies, not unlike protection services such as the Pinkerton Agency, advertised in the newspapers. The best-known agency for spies—the most notorious, to my mind—was the Railway Audit and Inspection Company. The name originated in the early days of railroading when the company had been formed to supply railroads with spies to check up on conductors who pocketed cash fares paid on the train, but the company had come a long way since its early days. By now it was supplying spies for all occasions. Two labor-spy experiences are still fresh in my mind.

The first concerned a man named George Kaufmann—at least, he called himself that. He could have been the prototype for *The Spy Who Came in from the Cold.* Short and shabby, with a narrow white face, he wore glasses so thick that they resembled magnifying lenses. I never knew where he lived. Whenever he wanted to get in touch with me, he would telephone my office and meet me on a downtown Philadelphia street corner so that our encounters would appear accidental. Kaufmann was perfectly willing to be a double agent. Although paid by Railway Audit to spy on the Hosiery Workers, he could also tell us of the employers' strategy in fighting the union. We paid him twenty dollars each for copies of the reports he sent to Railway Audit and money on a sliding scale for whatever information he could supply us about the employers' plans. We in Hosiery also employed Kaufmann some years later to make reports on the organizing possibilities at newly established mills, and his reports, I'm sorry to say, were often superior to those by members of our own staff. He was an extremely hard-working spy, much more experienced than our own average organizer.

My second labor-spy experience of those days involved Carl Holderman, a member of the National Executive Committee of the AFL, then serving as business agent for several branches of the Hosiery Workers in northern New Jersey.

One day in the fall of 1929 Carl was visited in his office in Paterson, New Jersey, by a well-dressed man with the appearance of a higher-type salesman. His name was George Stevens, and he carried credentials purporting to show that he represented the American Bankers Association. He explained that he would like Carl's advice on what plants might be in for union trouble so that the bankers would be able to make better judgments on loans. For this "advice" Carl was to be paid $150 a month.

There was just enough larceny in this proposal as it stood to make it seem logical, but Carl realized it would have even more logic if Stevens was really in the employ of the Railway Audit Company. So he played along, telling Stevens he'd have to consult with his boss. Immediately after Stevens left, Carl called the national office of the Hosiery Workers in Philadelphia and told William Smith, our secretary-treasurer, and me about the proposal. We decided to try to trap Stevens.

Carl had been one of the very first people in the labor movement to impress on me the necessity of making friends with local politicians whenever possible—a practice he invariably followed himself—so it was no accident that he had hired, as local attorney for the union in Paterson, a man who was also a city magistrate. After Carl had informed Smith and me of Stevens's proposal, he called in the attorney who told him that his course of action was perfectly simple. The state of New Jersey had a law making it a misdemeanor to offer a bribe to a trade-union official.

When Stevens returned with his money for Carl, a city detective was hiding in the coat closet. Stevens played it smart. When he was arrested in the act of handing the money to Carl, he refused to say a single word. After a couple of days in jail, a lawyer for the Railway Audit Company bailed Stevens out. The case was stalled through the courts for a year until everyone except us had forgotten about it; then it was transferred from Passaic County, of which Paterson is the county seat, to Hudson County, of which Jersey City is the county seat, which was being run by the notorious Frank ("I am the Boss") Hague. Railway Audit paid a five-hundred-dollar fine for Stevens without his ever appearing in court, and that was the end of that—except that Carl Holderman obtained Stevens's picture from the Paterson police. We ran it all through the labor press.

What inspired me to attack the problem of labor spies (for Railway Audit was only the best known of a number of such agencies) by legislative means was a bill that had been introduced in the House of Representatives in Washington by Victor Berger of Milwaukee, first socialist member of the House. The bill (which was not passed) would have required all civilian espionage agents and undercovermen to register with the State Departments in the various states; the registration rolls would have been open to public inspection.

I managed to get similar bills introduced into the state legislatures of Pennsylvania and New Jersey through the good offices of two friendly members of the lower houses, and I was able to push the cause by writing pieces for a weekly newspaper in the northeastern part of Philadelphia. I wrote a number of rather libelous stories about the labor-spy operations of the big hosiery mill owners, and while I heard that in private meetings the owners soundly damned the union, they never brought any court action against us. This was not exactly a piece of luck, for the mill owners undoubtedly knew that they would have won the suit and that the damages could have bankrupted the union, but the owners were too afraid of what we knew to take us into court.

In respect to pushing the labor-spy bills in Pennsylvania and New Jersey, I'm sorry to confess that one of our minor union officials was guilty of bribery. A clerk for a hearing committee on the bills asked for and got one hundred dollars to get the bill scheduled for consideration. I hit the ceiling when I heard the story. Apart from the basic question of morality, there are a number of pragmatic arguments against bribery. For one thing, it's illegal. For another, it's generally a waste of money. If you have the political muscle, you can accomplish your legislative aims legitimately, and paying a bribe isn't necessary; if you don't have the political muscle, you can't accomplish your aims anyway, and the money is wasted.

I was also angry over our role in the one-hundred-dollar bribe because I understood the political realities in New Jersey and Pennsylvania as well as any man at union headquarters. It was, in my opinion, a tossup as to which state was more politically corrupt. In Pennsylvania, the machine run by Boies Penrose, which had given that state its original foul political reputation, had been taken over (on Penrose's death in 1921) by William S. Vare, to whom the United States Senate refused a seat when he was elected in 1926. The amount of money Vare had spent for his election (a reported $5 million, comparable today to a senator's spending $50 million) staggered even the wealthiest and most conservative members of the Senate.

I had seen the Vare machine operate even down to the street corner. In those days, in northeast Philadelphia, working males stood around on the street corner of a Sunday morning, right after church, just to have a lazy talk. It was not at all unusual for a police paddy wagon to drive up and take them to the local police station where they would all be charged with "loitering." Generally, within half an hour, the local Vare ward heeler—or committeeman, as he was officially known—would get the men released on a "copy of the charges"—the form used by the sergeant at the police station for the names of those arrested and their alleged offenses. Such harassment by the Vare machine was intended to pressure the workers to register Republican, to vote Republican, to be in the good graces of the local "committeeman."

Along with the labor-spy bills on which we at Hosiery got hearings both in Trenton and Harrisburg, we were very active in our support of the Berger bill in Washington, which involved us in a serious dispute with the top AFL leadership. Basically, our way of supporting the bill was to buttonhole the congressmen we knew to get our views before the hearing committee. But that the top AFL leadership of the day was almost as conservative as Henry Cabot Lodge and almost as anti-socialist as the National Association of Manufacturers became manifest in the leadership's opposition to the Berger bill. This seemed senseless to me, since Berger could never have been elected to Congress without the backing of the AFL's own unions in Milwaukee and the financial aid of the Jewish unions in New York. In addition, the AFL leadership should have understood as well as we the threat to the whole labor-union movement that the widespread use of labor spies posed. But the innate conservatism of the top AFL hierarchy influenced them to conclude that Berger's socialism should not be supported.

Although the Berger bill was not passed, our efforts were not entirely in vain. The mere introduction of his bill, and ours, served to establish an atmosphere favorable to their eventual acceptance. In other words, even with a just cause, it is never, in my experience, possible to achieve instant reform. Generally, an abuse persists because the atmosphere of society encourages it or at least tolerates it. To end the abuse one must change the attitude of the society.

Despite our initial failure to obtain anti-labor-spy legislation then, we turned our efforts to move against another labor abuse, also all but forgotten today—the so-called yellow-dog contract, which required a worker hired at a plant to sign an agreement not to join a union. Not only labor men today but some of our best social historians tend to underestimate the widespread fear that this sort of contract evoked in hundreds of thousands of American workers. Some historians give the impression that the yellow-dog contract was confined pretty much to the coal-mining industry; this is not so. It was just as vicious a weapon in the hosiery industry, and it affected far more workers.

What made the yellow-dog contract so effective against union organizing was that the courts of those days were as antilabor as the employers, the newspapers, or the police.

Again and again, United States district courts upheld the validity of the yellow-dog contracts, though they were patently in violation of the basic Constitutional guarantees of free speech and association. A worker facing the very real possibility of going to jail or being fined for joining a union is not very likely to do so. The federal injunction was a massive and all-pervasive weapon against labor in those days.

In my capacity as public-relations director for the Hosiery Workers, I found what I thought was a good news story. I had discovered a refinement of the yellow-dog contract that was being put into effect by the Real Silk Hosiery Mills at Indianapolis, Indiana, and I labeled it the "Double Decker Yellow Dog." Unfortunately, almost no one knew what I was talking about. Because so many minors in their late teens were going to work in the hosiery mills in those boom days (sales of full-fashioned silk stockings boomed through most of the Depression), the Real Silk people had the parents of underage workers countersign the yellow-dog contracts so that if the youngster joined the union, the parent could be sent to jail.

The Real Silk people posed a triple threat for us in Hosiery, the first part of which was their very location. Indianapolis was one of the most conservative—not to say hidebound—cities in the North. Both the local and United States courts there were extremely reactionary. (In 1927, the governor of Indiana and the mayor of Indianapolis were indicted for accepting bribes from the Ku Klux Klan.) The second part of the problem was that Real Silk had built a very strong company union. The third, and most paradoxical, was that the company was so successful.

It is almost axiomatic that a union does not enjoy much of a bargaining position with an unsuccessful company. But Real Silk's system of door-to-door peddling of hosiery at marked-down prices had become so successful that it was jeopardizing the business of other manufacturers. If Real Silk came to dominate the entire market, it would put some of the companies with which we had contracts out of business, which would mean a great loss to us in dues-paying members. Also, by enforcing their yellow-dog (and "Double Decker Yellow Dog") contracts in the courts, Real Silk was able to pay considerably less than the going wage that we had established in the plants around Philadelphia. Our manufacturers were beginning to ask, "How long are you going to let Real Silk get away with this?"

At this point Louis Budenz approached me with a first-class idea. Budenz, as I have mentioned, was a brilliant but intellectually eccentric chap, moving from one "cause" to another. Having started out as a welfare case worker in St. Louis, he had then become field secretary for Roger Baldwin's American Civil Liberties Union. Then he had set up a committee, financed with funds from various liberal unions such as Hosiery, to publish a monthly magazine called *Labor Age* in which he belabored the theme that the AFL had become an obsolete mechanism by which to achieve social progress. I was pretty much in total agreement. Budenz also arranged conferences, issued manifestoes and press releases, and generally tried to fan the fires of revolt within the AFL. I had resumed my fairly close relationship with Budenz when I recommended that Hosiery hire him to oversee a strike at the Allen-A mills at Kenosha, Wisconsin. The Allen-A strike involved some three hundred workers—no small affair in the hosiery industry of that day—and the issue was what became known as the "two-machine system." Essentially this was a management scheme to dilute the amount of skilled (and therefore more highly paid) labor in the industry.

Up until then standard practice in mills called for one machine, one man. The legging machines of those days (the machines that knit the leg part of the stocking) knit eighteen legs of stockings simultaneously. Because the whole secret of the success of the full-fashioned hosiery industry depended on knitting the silk to enhance the curves of the female leg from the ankle to the top of the thigh, these machines were terribly complicated. They were thirty feet long and eight feet high, and each had nine thousand needles. When the legs were knit, the stockings were transferred to a second machine that sewed the seams up the back; then to a "footing" machine, which sewed the feet onto the stockings; and finally they were dyed and then dried on a "boarding" machine, which held highly polished steel forms on which the stockings were placed to pass them through an electric oven.

The knitting machines were placed facing away from each other so that two legging knitters (called "leggers") worked back-to-back in the same aisle. The knitters worked on a piecework system (traditional in the industry); they would time the operation of the machines so that while one machine was actually knitting, the other would be finished, and both knitters could cooperate in shifting its bars (with the finished legs attached) to the successive machines, thus jointly increasing their production.

One of the important duties of the "legger" involved keeping the thousands of needles in each machine in exact alignment by the use of a special pair of pliers that he kept in a leather holder on his belt. If even one needle fell out of alignment, it would affect the quality of the knit, and the needles were forever doing just that.

Allen-A proposed that one "legger" operate two machines, with the assistance of two unskilled helpers. The helpers could transfer the finished legs to the seaming and footing machines with relative ease—it was a rather uncomplicated job—but neither of them would have the experience to be trusted with lining up the needles.

As a solution to this problem, I asked Morris Llewellyn Cooke to do a time-motion study on the company's proposal, but, as with so many similar issues, rational debate gave way to bickering about management "prerogatives" and union "infringements." The study was never made, and the union went on strike.

Getting the union to hire Budenz to supervise the Allen-A strike was a great boon to me—my presence was not required—and it also gave Budenz a chance to show his own considerable abilities, which included a talent for leadership and an ability to get along with factory workers.

He not only did a remarkable job in maintaining the spirit and solidarity of the striking hosiery workers but also built a measurable amount of support in the community as a whole—Kenosha in those days was hardly what would be called a "labor town." The big plant in the city was the totally unorganized Nash Motor Company. Some of the sparks that Budenz struck off at Allen-A inspired many of the Nash workers to join our picket lines, which established an atmosphere that led, only a few years later, to the organization of the Nash plant itself.

When two-hundred-odd strikers were arrested (under the court interpretation of the yellow-dog agreements) and received sentences of thirty days each in the federal detention center in Milwaukee, Budenz talked the prison officials into letting him take a picture of the group standing outside the prison gates. We were able to get the picture into a hundred-odd newspapers throughout the country. In addition, two of the strikers were a remarkably attractive set of twin girls, twenty years old and Scottish, whose parents were strong supporters of the union. We sent these girls on a nationwide speaking tour, mainly to labor conventions and central labor-union meetings, dressed in their plaid skirts and tam-o'-shanters and doing the Highland fling after they'd talked, from which we received a considerable amount of publicity. Our branch of the Hosiery Workers in Milwaukee, Branch Six, held a gala reception for the strikers when they were released, which made quite a splash in the newspapers throughout the Midwest.

In the Real Silk situation, however, Budenz reminded me that he and I had both been close to James Meyers, the labor secretary of the National Council of Churches of Christ in America, the central federation of Protestant churches in America. A few years earlier the council had conducted a survey of labor conditions in the American steel industry and had published a report that for many years was a classic document. Budenz now suggested that we get in touch with Meyers and ask the council to prepare a similar study on the institution of the company union, namely, that of the Real Silk company.

The council's study, when finished, was by all odds the best study of labor relations in a company up to that time. The Hosiery Workers spent a good deal of money (for a union that size), and I kept my small staff busy full time for several weeks in our Philadelphia headquarters mailing out copies of the report to everyone of consequence, even to those people listed in *Who's Who.*

Both the Real Silk and the Allen-A situations ended amorphously. We were not able to organize Real Silk until much later (not until after they had spent far more of their corporate money on lawyers' fees and publicity costs to fight us than they would ever have spent in increased labor costs if we had organized them in the first place), and we were never able to do a time-motion study of Allen-A's "double machine" system. The introduction of nylon thread so revolutionized the entire knitting industry that a study of silk-knitting machines became academic.

Since in both situations federal injunctions were used by

the companies to enforce yellow-dog contracts, we in Hosiery were convinced that the court injunction was being used as an anti-labor weapon with increasingly ominous frequency. Even today I don't understand why the companies applied for federal injunctions. State court injunctions were certainly as effective, frequently more brutal, and they would have achieved the same results without the national attention that federal injunctions drew.

Nonetheless, that is what happened. By this time many people in labor besides me had come to realize that the power of the federal courts in this field would have to be curbed by legislative action—by the Congress. The law that eventually achieved that, and for the enactment of which I worked so long, is known as the Norris-LaGuardia Act. As is so frequently the case with bills in Congress, neither George W. Norris, the fiercely independent senator from Nevada, nor Fiorello H. LaGuardia, later the feisty mayor of New York City but then in the House, were concerned with the bill at the start.

The bill actually had had its beginnings in 1928 in the mind of Andrew Furuseth, one of the towering and tragic figures of the American labor movement. A tough, dedicated, singleminded and self-educated Norwegian immigrant seaman (a "sea lawyer," they called him), Furuseth had begun his labor career around the turn of the century organizing his fellow sailors on the rough and murderous docks of San Francisco and had risen to become president of the once-proud AFL International Seamen's Union. (A series of disastrous strikes against slashes in the seamen's wages following the end of World War I reduced Furuseth's union's membership from a peak of 100,000 to one so small that it wasn't even listed in annual reports; Furuseth's position of power on the AFL executive committee was slowly but effectively cut from under him.)

Furuseth had had very early experience with the court injunction as a weapon against labor organizing, and some of his words still re-echo through history:

> You can put me in jail, but you cannot give me narrower quarters than as a seaman I have always had. You cannot give me coarser food than I have always eaten. You cannot make me lonelier than I have always been.

In 1925 he was still fighting the good fight, and he wrote a basic draft of proposals that he thought, if properly framed and passed by Congress, would destroy the power of the court injunction against labor.

To introduce these proposals in the Congress, Furuseth went to another Norwegian immigrant, Sen. Henrik Shipstead of Minnesota. Shipstead did not have the political power in the Senate to get his bill past the hearing committee stage, but he did attract the attention of Senator Norris, along with Senators Tom Walsh of Montana and John J. Blaine of Wisconsin. They rewrote the bill and urged LaGuardia to introduce it in the House. (The rewriting of congressional bills is such a complicated art that I'm surprised law schools do not teach courses in it. It is not so simple, as in this case, as deciding that the principle of using the court injunction to break strikes and to prevent union organizing should be ended. That is just the beginning. The bill must then be rephrased with an eye toward passage through Congress; it must take into account what effect it will have on various state and local conditions—which, if serious enough, could ensure its defeat—and it must be written so that it cannot be interpreted in such a way as to bring about results never originally intended. Such a process can take months.)

In addition to Norris, Walsh, and Blaine numerous others began to take an interest in the Shipstead Bill. The top hierarchy of the AFL had suddenly begun to realize, as they had not with the "labor spy" issue, that continued court enforcement of yellow-dog contracts could wreck the whole union. In addition, some leading members of the legal profession were beginning to become seriously alarmed at this legal subversion of the courts.

Dr. Felix Frankfurter of the Harvard Law School (later, of

course, to become a justice of the Supreme Court) together with a colleague, Professor Nathan Greene, wrote in the *Harvard Law Review:*

> The extraordinary remedy of the injunction has become the ordinary legal remedy, almost the sole remedy. An ordinary employer seeks an injunction for the most part while a strike is in progress. His attorney files a bill of equity in a trial court having jurisdiction, usually seeking out an injunction judge. [Meaning one who is known to be favorable to granting the injunction.] The bill . . . alleges the union's intent to commit irreparable damages and pleads for relief. The union is afforded neither notice nor hearing. The judge simply issues an ex parte temporary restraining order by affixing his signature to the draft submitted by the company. The order invariably applies to the union, its agents and attorneys, and "all persons in aid or in connection with them"; often it covers "all persons whomsoever." It commonly prohibits the use of force, coercion or intimidation by the union, prevents picketing, bars boycotts, trespass, the use of the word "scab," the payment of strike benefits, sometimes forbids the union to hold meetings or the workers to strike. . . .

With powerful lawyers of Frankfurter's status on our side; senators of the stature of Norris, Walsh, Shipstead, and Blaine; and the top level of the AFL—the future of anti-injunction legislation began to look pretty rosy.

I decided to muster all the political power I could in Pennsylvania to give support to the Norris-LaGuardia Act, and to this end I helped set up the "National Committee on Labor Injunction," which was to include not just labor people but everyone of real influence who would assist us.

I was able to raise some money from the Hosiery Workers to defray the expenses of this committee, and I was able to persuade Alexander Fleischer to become its secretary. Fleischer was the wealthy owner of a carpet company that had been in his family for three generations. He was a world traveler, an amateur art collector, and a liberal who had only recently been appointed chairman of the Pennsylvania State Planning Board by Governor Pinchot.

To kick off Pennsylvania support for the "Committee on Labor Injunction," we decided to hold a fancy fund-raising dinner in Philadelphia. I wanted Professor Frankfurter as the principal speaker, but when I told his secretary at Harvard Law School the details of my request, I was never able to get Frankfurter to return my calls. A number of years later I ran into him at the funeral services for Mrs. Pinchot in Washington at St. John's Episcopal Church across from the White House, and while we were chatting, I reminded him of the event. I had the nerve to say, "And where were you when I needed you?"

"Oh, my God," was all he answered. By then I had come to well understand Frankfurter's single-minded ambition. A professor of law at Harvard who has his heart set on the Supreme Court is not going to jeopardize that ambition.

Lacking Frankfurter, I set about looking for another "name" speaker. This turned out to be a youthful woman named Josephine Roche, rich, pretty, a recent graduate of Smith College, a social worker, and very much in the news. She had inherited the Rocky Mountain Coal and Iron Company, and in going through the books of the company, she had found a most explicit list of expenditures for arms and explosives to be used against strikers and union organizers. She had written about this in the *Survey*, a monthly magazine for social workers, and the story had been reprinted by the *New York World*.

I was not surprised at the success that Josephine Roche's appearance brought to this dinner; what did surprise me was the entirely unexpected appearance at the dinner of John P. Frey. Frey was at that time chairman of the Metal Trades Department of the AFL, president of the Molders International Union, and member of the AFL executive council.

I could hardly have been more surprised if William Green himself had shown up unannounced and slipped into a sixth-row seat. Frey's appearance meant that the very top brass of the AFL was really interested in what we were doing. At the end of Josephine Roche's speech, when questions from the floor were invited and Frey introduced himself, I could hear the gasps going through the hall.

Later, I heard from Florence Thorne at the AFL headquarters in Washington (she had been Samuel Gompers's secretary in the old days) that Frey had delivered a glowing report of our meeting to his fellow members of the executive council.

As a consequence of this, I found that for a long while I was a fair-haired boy around Massachusetts Avenue and 9th Street—the old headquarters of the AFL—even more so after the Norris-LaGuardia Act was finally passed. For years after, whenever I met Bill Green around Washington, he would throw his arm across my shoulders and pump my hand.

Chapter Eight

PUBLIC HOUSING today is so familiar a part of our urban scene, so much a part of our way of thinking, that it is hard to realize that only a little over a generation ago—forty years ago—even the concept of using public funds to build housing was almost totally unknown in the United States. Neither the average American citizen, businessman, or politician had ever heard of public housing. You were laughed at for even suggesting the concept. Use tax dollars to build housing? Taxes were for highways, hospitals, schools, and battleships.

During World War I, the federal government set up a US Housing Corporation to ease the housing shortage in several cities in which the sudden expansion of industries had created a serious crisis, and there had been a number of similarly futile efforts thereafter. But there were then few people in this country who either had heard of public housing or knew that public housing projects already existed in some European countries—Austria, for example—and these people were mostly specialists in the field, architects and city planners.

I remember very clearly what got me interested in public housing. It was a sheer visceral reaction to the sight of human suffering.

It occurred during the Hoover administration when I was working for the Hosiery Workers. Prior to the Depression, hosiery workers were faring as well as, or better than, any group of workers in the United States. Those were the days, in the mid-twenties, of short skirts and silk stockings, and the hosiery manufacturers, to make their product sexier, had designed "full-fashioned" silk hosiery. In a matter of only months this kind of stocking changed from a luxury to something that every nubile young woman, whether shopgirl, stenographer, or debutante, simply had to own. Indeed, the distinguished Cole Porter wrote a musical comedy called *Silk Stockings*. The demand for full-fashioned hosiery was practically inexhaustible, its manufacture required highly skilled workers, and the pay was good.

The hosiery workers under the influence of this prosperity were, to my knowledge, the first of all factory hands to break the pattern of living in what were called "half streets" in the Philadelphia of those days.

Until then, virtually all industrial workers simply accepted life in such "half streets," in which there were no back yards, and no front yards, either. Builders would construct a row of houses flush with the edge of the sidewalks on one street; behind them they left enough room for an alley for garbage trucks. The houses facing on the parallel street would back onto the same alley. Two to four families lived in each house.

But in Philadelphia in the twenties, hosiery workers began to leave these houses for modest bungalows with space for a garden located a short distance from the factory areas where the air seemed cleaner. Workers in other hosiery centers—in Dover and Boonton, New Jersey, in Fort Wayne and Milwaukee—followed suit, but Philadelphia was by all odds the largest of the silk hosiery manufacturing centers, and the change was most noticeable there. Then came the Depression.

It is difficult to believe that we could have lived through the Depression without revolution and blood in the streets. Not that there wasn't bloodshed; there was little, however, considering the desperate mood of the country. Moreover, there are analogies that can be drawn between those days and today. Dickens's "It was the best of times, it was the worst of times" is as applicable today as it was then. People felt that the government, specifically Mr. Hoover, had failed them; that, to use the jargon of the soapbox orators and the *Daily Worker*, the bankers had betrayed them, the stock market was the venal tool of the capitalist system, the big corporations were destroying the working class. There were threats of revolution, open demands for the overthrow of the government, hunger marches, riots in the streets and in the parks.

But in the midst of our despair there was a feeling of comradeship that came from the fact that—unlike today—just about every family, except for the likes of the Morgans and the Mellons, knew the real impact of the Depression.

After all, at the height of the Depression in 1933, thirteen million—a quarter of the working force—were unemployed, and even the lucky ones with a job had only to look at the newspapers to wonder, Will I be next? The fear of being unemployed gnawed one's insides at night. Newspaper pictures and movie newsreels constantly reminded everyone of bread lines and soup kitchens, the riots of a thousand men fighting for fifty jobs, men and women selling apples for a nickel apiece on street corners—a kind of charity itself since apples sold in the stores for a nickel a pound—men wearing signs reading, "I'm for sale for any job at any wage."

Today's society is so affluent, as John Kenneth Galbraith has phrased it, that it is impossible to convey what living in the Depression was like to those who didn't endure it. Human experience is nontransferable.

For me one of the most traumatic of all experiences then was seeing what happened to the young hosiery workers who had broken out of the "half street" pattern of life. Most of them were about my age, and, like me, most of them had small children. They had sunk practically all their capital in down payments on their little homes, generally with some private builder who was working on speculation. They had whacking great mortgages, and when they missed a couple of payments, out they went into the streets, evicted by a city marshall. Their equity in their homes was wiped out, more often than not their furniture was repossessed, they had no place to live, they had no jobs.

As union representative, I would steel myself to visit these families, for I knew I would find the kids crying, the mothers covering their faces with their aprons, the young fathers white-faced and lost. But sometimes I couldn't go. I would just walk around, unable to speak, ashamed of myself for having a job.

Returning home from these heart-rending scenes, night after night, I grew more convinced that labor unions, labor people, simply couldn't allow such suffering to continue. Sooner or later they would simply have to do something about housing.

There existed also around Philadelphia in those days men who felt similarly about housing, but whose knowledge of it was greater than mine. One was an organizer for the Amalgamated Clothing Workers (ACW) named Leo Kryzski, who was based in Milwaukee. There he had been sheriff for several terms when the socialists controlled the city government, but he had been sent to Pennsylvania to organize "runaway" shops that had moved from the Amalgamated's jurisdiction in Milwaukee, New York, and other cities to take advantage of unorganized rural workers in Pennsylvania.

Leo, a short while before, had made a trip to Europe, and in Vienna he had been very much impressed by the Karl Marx Hof, a huge workers' housing project. He had taken a great many photographs there, and back in Philadelphia, at the drop of the word "housing," Leo would bring them out and deliver a spirited lecture on the feasibility of Americans emulating the Austrians. Leo was one of the men who got the labor movement to begin to think about the viability of low-cost housing.

An incident that occurred at that time showed me what a long hard road lay ahead. In those days, we in labor were ideologically thrashing around, completely overwhelmed by the economic disaster that had overtaken us and the country, talking in the shibboleths of socialism and at the same time looking for "good" capitalists—capitalists with soul, so to speak. I got Governor Pinchot to introduce me to George Horace Lorrimer, then editor of the *Saturday Evening Post*, soon to become president of the Curtis Publishing Company. Even during the Depression the company was sound, and it owned a substantial amount of Philadelphia real estate. Lorrimer listened to my idea that his company finance a public housing project on one of its building sites, then simply smiled and shook his head. It was only an incident, but it convinced me that we weren't going to receive much help from private enterprise for public housing.

Another Philadelphian I met in those days, who was to play an extremely important role in public housing, was the architect Oskar Stonorov. (I am grieved to say that Stonorov was killed on May 9, 1970, in the plane crash that also took the lives of other old friends, Walter P. Reuther, president of the United Auto Workers (UAW), and his wife Mae. All were on their way to visit a UAW Family Education Center near Onaway, Michigan, that had been designed by Oskar.)

Oskar was a big, burly man, a sort of russet bear, full of the zest and lust of life. When he talked—which was a good deal of the time—you could hear him for a full city block, and his laugh carried even farther. His forebears had been members of the czar's court in Russia, and he had been raised in Frankfurt, Germany, where his mother had taken him after the Russian Revolution in 1917. As a young man, he had studied architecture at the University of Florence in Italy and at the École Polytechnique in Zurich and had been a pupil of both the French architect Le Corbusier and the French sculptor Aristide Maillol.

Frankly, much as I came to esteem and admire him later, at first I thought Oskar bumptious. I didn't take him very seriously. Only a few days later I recognized that I should have.

At that first meeting, after I had learned that Oskar was an architect, though not yet licensed to practice in Pennsyl-

vania, I mentioned to him the subject of workers' housing. He instantly bubbled over with twenty minutes' worth of enthusiasm about workers' housing in Europe. His own ideas on the subject were considerable. Still, I left with the impression that Oskar simply talked a lot.

A few days later, on Labor Day, 1930, the Hosiery Workers were picnicking on a vacant lot in the heart of the industrial section of Philadelphia. I still remember what a lovely, lazy summer day it was. People were really more interested in eating and relaxing than in the seemingly endless speeches being made in favor of the socialist candidates in the forthcoming election. About halfway through the speaking program Oskar arrived, voice booming and seeming half again life size. I had only talked to him for about twenty minutes earlier, but what he'd done in the interim, I learned later, was typical of him.

Oskar had a partner, Alfred Kastner, who was fully as offbeat a character as Stonorov. He had been a much-decorated flier in the German Air Force in World War I and had furthered his education afterward on the German equivalent of the GI bill. He had learned architecture under Walter Gropius at the famed Bauhaus school, and had emigrated to the United States for the simple purpose of availing himself of greater opportunities.

I was always sorry that Alfred and Oskar later broke up their partnership, but the reason was not hard to discover. Despite the vast difference in their backgrounds, they were too much alike. They were both big men physically, they were both filled with a zest for living, they were both extremely fond of talking in sonorous tones, and they were both extremely opinionated. I admired the opinions of both even though—as frequently happened—they were completely at odds.

Oskar and Alfred Kastner had drawn up all the preliminary plans for an entire workers' housing project. They had made a cardboard model of it that Oskar had brought with him mounted on a board. That put an effective end to the political speeches for the day. Oskar and his housing model became the focus of attention; people crowded around him in the sunshine asking questions. He must have talked for an hour.

The climate of the times was against us. Low-cost housing was still thought of as some sort of socialist experiment being attempted in Europe. Few union leaders whom I knew took it at all seriously. But the image of the evicted hosiery workers was still fixed in my mind, and men like Kryzski and Stonorov were making the dream of workers' housing seem not so visionary after all.

And there were beginning to be some little breakthroughs. One was a survey that we—the Hosiery Workers—made in 1932–33. The actual work was done by six graduate students at Bryn Mawr College; directed by the college, it was sponsored and paid for by the Hosiery Workers.

The survey was tremendously important from a historical point of view. The poll technique in other fields was not new. The first political one was held in 1824 when a newspaper, the *Harrisburg Pennsylvanian,* polled its readers to learn whether they were going to vote for Clay, Jackson, Adams, or Crawford for president; and the first market survey was done in 1912, for a breakfast food. Ours was the first on a socioeconomic problem, and it set the pattern for all that followed—for example, the WPA's "Real Inventory and Property Survey," which was incorporated into the United States Census.

The idea of taking the survey grew from a conversation I had with Stonorov. When I mentioned to him that we seemed to be failing to persuade people with influence about the validity of the low-cost housing concept, he said that we weren't documenting our case sufficiently. Between us, we worked out the sort of statistical material that we would need; then I went to Emil Rieve. He agreed to have the union finance it, provided it didn't cost too much. It's generally that way, and I say it in kindness. Spare no expense planning for the future, provided it doesn't cost too much.

I then talked to a friend named William Jeanes, a gaunt,

lanky Philadelphia Quaker engineer, millionaire, and philanthropist. Jeanes, Oskar, and I decided to take our problem to Dr. Susan Kingsbury at Bryn Mawr. Dr. Kingsbury, a vibrant white-haired woman then just entering her sixties, had received her Ph.D. from Columbia in 1905, and she was both professor of social economy and director of the graduate department of social economy and social research. She agreed to help us.

The survey that Dr. Kingsbury supervised for us—with her six graduate students in the working districts of Philadelphia, taking notes on pads of paper—provided us with the answers to a lot of pragmatic questions that apparently had not been asked before. Focus sleeping quarters near the living room, not the kitchen. (The kitchen tends to be the noisy center of activity in a working home.) Have the bathroom close to the kitchen. (The flushing sound is least noticeable, and the same drain can be used.) Provide storage space for dangerous cleaning agents like ammonia up high so that small children cannot reach them. No more than two children to a bedroom, unless very young. Have an outside window over the kitchen sink so that the housewife can look out while doing her chores.

My wife Kate was absolutely invaluable in helping develop the survey. It was she who framed many of the questions included in the planning of facilities for wives and young children—the need for playground areas with *real dirt* for digging and getting filthy in (sand can be substituted) in which children can use their imaginations, rather than formal ones in which they are restricted to the traditional slides and swings. It was Kate, also, who virtually assumed the planning of the kitchens—where the sink should be, the refrigerator, and so on.

Out of this survey came most of the standards for the first real workers' housing project in the United States, which we in Hosiery built. These were the Carl Mackley Houses, even today a model for public housing—four-story buildings with plenty of grass and play space, community rooms, a swimming pool. (The project was named for a hosiery worker killed by Philadelphia police during a strike.) Since Emil Rieve was as aware as I of the need for housing, there had been no trouble in getting union support for the project.

The first step had been to find a site. As mentioned, before the Depression the Hosiery Workers had been one of the richest unions, for its size, in the nation. Branch One, the Philadelphia local, was the biggest in the country. Our lawyer was Michael Francis Doyle, who had been attorney for Sir Roger Casement. (Sir Roger was the Ulster Protestant knighted for his services in exposing the appalling conditions under which rubber workers labored in British African colonies, in which Casement was British consular officer. Later, he became an ardent Irish nationalist, and when he secretly traveled to Germany in 1916 by German submarine to find support for the Irish cause, he was, on his return, stripped of his title by the British and hanged.) Doyle, as counsel for the Hosiery Workers in the booming days of the mid-twenties, had advised the union to put its funds into what were then regarded as the safest of all investments, real estate mortgages. With the Depression came the foreclosures, and the union was about to be forced to sell its holdings at considerable loss when Doyle and William Jeanes proposed a deal whereby the Hosiery Workers would relinquish its equity in three square blocks in south Philadelphia for clear title to one square block in north Philadelphia, within walking distance of most of the major hosiery mills. That was to be our site.

How we in the union financed the project, in the eyes of a hardheaded businessman, would be straight out of Alice in Wonderland.

We simply had to have a loan from the Public Works Administration (PWA). The cost of the project designed by Stonorov and Kastner was estimated at just over $1.1 million, and the loan we wanted from the PWA was $1 million.

All through the early thirties I had been traveling to Washington once a week, partly to lobby for the interests of the Hosiery Workers and partly on a consultant's job for the Resettlement Administration. I was so green in those days that I didn't even know my way around the office buildings on the Hill. One of the first things that Congress had passed as part of the National Recovery Act was a public works bill, designed to create jobs by financing the construction of a variety of public projects.

One night I was heading back from Washington to Philadelphia with an hour or so to kill. I could see from the lights that the Senate was still in session, so I made my way to the visitors' gallery; after I had listened to the debate for only a few minutes, I almost fell out of the gallery. Sen. David I. Walsh of Massachusetts was arguing that the government, as part of the public works bill, should be given the right to build public housing.

The reason that I was so surprised is that I had done my homework on Dave. The first thing a lobbyist must learn is the background of all the congressmen: what his district is like, whether it's dairy farmers or steel workers, the interests he represents, the kind of people who elect him, the pressures to which he's likely to be susceptible.

Walsh had been the first Roman Catholic elected governor of Massachusetts, then United States senator. His father and mother had emigrated from Ireland to the small city of Leominster, forty miles west-northwest of Boston, and there Walsh had been born. His father had been a hornsmith. (In the 1880s combs were made from the horns of slaughtered cattle, and the men who heated the horns, softened them in boiling oil, and hammered them flat on anvils, were called hornsmiths.) Walsh once said that his father never made more than twelve dollars a week, but on it he raised a family of ten; he died when Dave was twelve. His mother then opened a boarding house for carpet-mill workers, and through a combination of diligence, hard work, and every member of the family contributing to the common welfare, she had managed to put three boys through law school.

But Walsh was no more simple a person than any other senator. At first, in my own naïveté, I had simply written him off as an Irish Catholic "pol" from Massachusetts. The first duty of every congressman, of course, is to get elected; the second is to get re-elected. But Massachusetts (Irish Catholic) politicians in those days were in rather bad repute.

Walsh to his dying day suffered from his own particular dichotomy. On the one hand, he himself had been poor, and the people who elected him were poor. Yet his upbringing and education through Holy Cross College and Boston University Law School had given him firm conviction in the precepts of self-help and self-improvement, as well as in the value of the private property that a successful man accumulates.

When it came to public money for housing, therefore, Dave Walsh was torn between his sure knowledge that the poor needed housing and his conviction that the Lord helps him who helps himself. "The government has no business whatsoever," he once said, "in building homes for persons in low-income groups, except for those whose incomes are so small that they live in hovels. . . . We must confine ourselves to slum clearance and to people who live in slums."

If Walsh was a liberal, he was very low-key; nonetheless, here he was in the Senate that night advocating public money for public housing, and he was the first senator I had heard do it. I went out of the visitors' gallery feeling a little dazed. All the way to Philadelphia I kept muttering, "Maybe this is it, maybe this is it." I could hardly wait for the next day to call Stonorov, Kastner, and Jeanes.

A few weeks after the Public Works Act was passed, incorporating Walsh's housing provision, I was in Washington on Hosiery Workers' business, and I was just finishing up at about eleven o'clock one night when Oskar showed up. I was wall-eyed with fatigue, but Oskar was bustling with energy.

"John," he said, "you remember about housing?"

I remember looking at him for a couple of seconds before I said, "Yes, I remember about housing."

"Well," Oskar said, "I've gotten to know the guy who heads up the housing division of Public Works. He's Robert Kohn, a fancy-pants New York architect but a good guy. Let's go see him."

"At this hour?"

"At this hour."

So Oskar called the Hay-Adams Hotel where Kohn was staying; he was asleep. Oskar woke him up, talked to him for a few minutes, and finally Kohn said, "Okay, goddamn it, for you bastards I'll get out of bed. Come on over."

We told him of the Carl Mackley project, and after we had talked for more than an hour, Kohn yawned and said. "Okay, I'm going back to bed. Give me a justification on this, and the specifications, and I'll set aside $1 million for you."

That was the step that financed the Carl Mackley Houses.

Since I'm not a businessman, I frankly admit that I didn't understand half of what was going on at the financial end. To qualify for the loan, the Hosiery Workers first had to establish a corporation, which was accomplished by Doyle. Emil Rieve was named president, and I was named secretary.

With the corporation duly recorded, the title to the site cleared, thirty thousand dollars cash that Bill Jeanes contributed for payments and other starting expenses, and the plans from Kastner and Stonorov, one fine day I walked out of the offices of the PWA's housing division in Washington with a United States Treasury check for one million dollars in my inside coat pocket. It was quite a day.

The next happiest day was at the ground-breaking ceremonies with Mrs. Cornelia Pinchot, the governor's wife, turning the first spadeful of earth. It was a gray, sullen day, and I can still see in my mind's eye Mrs. Pinchot's flaming red hair blowing in the wind. The ceremony was as elaborate as we could make it, for this was the first workers' housing project publicly financed in the United States, and it was one of the few major building projects of any kind in the entire nation.

There are two points to make about the Carl Mackley Houses. Our method of financing is not suitable to large-scale public housing projects; we learned that. Despite what today sounds like unbelievably low rents—two-room apartments started at $27 a month, five rooms at $52.50—the units turned out to be, in the end, too expensive for the average blue-collar hosiery worker and ended up being rented by white-collar people.

The second point is that into the contract with the builders, the Turner Construction Company, was written a no-strike provision, a standard feature of all public-housing agreements in the country today. It is a provision essential for public housing, and the reason must be obvious. The increase in costs that a strike might add to a project already being financed by public monies would be intolerable.

Another housing program with which I was closely involved was operated by the Resettlement Administration (RA). The Depression had, of course, struck hardest at the poorest, among them destitute sharecroppers evicted from their miserable holdings as a result of the crop-curtailment program devised by the Department of Agriculture to raise farm prices. Finally, the Department of Agriculture itself, under Secretary Henry Agard Wallace, recognized its own responsibility in the problem, and the RA was established. Rexford Tugwell, then best known as a great agrarian reformer (and one of the original "brain trusters"), was put in charge.

It sounded so delightfully simple: to build new homes in areas in which there were jobs—or, hopefully, might be—and where people could raise gardens to supplement low or irregular incomes, then move the homeless there.

One of the earliest projects was at Hightstown, New Jersey, where the RA resettled a colony of indigent Jewish immigrants who were supposed to raise poultry. The basic problem of the immigrants was that they knew absolutely nothing about the caring and raising of anything with feathers. They were mostly refugees from Germany, driven from their homeland by both the depression there and the rising tide of Nazism, and they were mostly tailors.

When the chicken-raising program turned out to be a disaster, the RA people running Hightstown decided that the best way to rescue them would be to establish a garment factory in the area. To this end they had approached David Dubinsky. Dubinsky then was an up-and-coming official in the ILGWU. While he was desperately anxious to find jobs for the refugees, he was smart enough to know that a garment factory in Hightstown was doomed before it started. The transportation costs alone would be prohibitive. Dubinsky was dead set against it.

To get him to change his mind, the Hightstown people got together a delegation to call on him. To head the delegation they were able to enlist Albert Einstein, newly arrived in this country and very concerned with the plight of fellow refugees.

When the delegation arrived, Dubinsky's secretary took one look and charged into Dubinsky's office crying: "Duvidal, Duvidal, Einstein is here!" (Duvidal was what his close associates called Dubinsky.)

Dubinsky invited the delegation in, and before he could say a word, Einstein—a shrewd man as well as a legendary physicist—launched into a flowery address about what a great man Dubinsky was, how the Jews looked to him for leadership, and could he possibly see his way clear to establishing a garment factory at Hightstown?

I'll never forget Dave's reply. He looked at Einstein and said, "Professor, you are without doubt the greatest star in the Jewish firmament. But"—and he shrugged—"but me, I know cloaks and suits."

Later, however, Dave gave in, with the greatest reluctance, and he was proved right. The factory was a flop—a pity from two standpoints. The refugees were again out of work, and eventually it meant the loss of the handsome factory building designed by Stonorov and Kastner.

One thing that was about to help those of us who were interested in a public-housing program was that about this time I was able to get three building trades leaders in Pennsylvania involved in public housing. Before the Depression this would not have been possible, basically because the concept of the trade-union movement then was still the old hanse or guild tradition of a group of skilled craftsmen banding together to protect their own economic interests. The entire basis of this thesis had been destroyed, as we can now see, by the arrival of mass production, in which the skilled machine eliminates the skilled worker, but how long its rituals would have continued without the Depression I don't know. However, the building trades were now faced with the fact that, with the country prostrate and no building at all going on, the unions and the workers alike would be penniless unless they improved the social conditions that had brought about this situation.

The men I got involved in public housing were John A. Phillips, president of the Pennsylvania state council of the AFL; James McDevitt, then head of the plasterers in Philadelphia and later head of the Committee on Political Education (COPE); and Charles Holopeter, president of the Camden, New Jersey, AFL council, who at that moment was an out-of-work plumber. But these men cut some ice in the labor movement, and they later became officers of the Labor Housing Conference, which was to be an important factor in getting the concept of public housing established in this country.

Two months after the Mackley Houses ground-breaking, in April 1935, an incident occurred that marked the beginning of a real breakthrough for housing. Bill Jeanes had bought a farm in Delaware that had gone to rack and ruin and was trying to rehabilitate it by taking small groups of friends down on weekends to help him, in return for board and room and hospitality, plant seedling trees or cut down brush. On this particular weekend, Kate and I were to have gone down with Bill and Stonorov and a woman named Catherine Bauer, but Kate and I hadn't been able to take off the time. We were just getting ready for bed in Flourtown on Sunday night when the other three came in, bubbling over with health and with a plan they had dreamed up.

Catherine Bauer, who became world-famous with her book *Modern Housing,* was a remarkable woman. (She later married William Wurster, dean of the School of Architecture at the University of California at Berkeley; she was killed in a hiking-trail accident in 1963.) With the profile of a hawk, she was not a conventional beauty, but she had an enormous amount of sex appeal—which she was perfectly willing to use on susceptible senators. She had a lucid, sparkling mind coupled with almost inexhaustible energy that enabled her to work sixteen hours a day, day after day, and she had unswervable drive.

Every Vassar girl worthy of the name back in those days had to serve a short term in Greenwich Village playing around with the communists, and Catherine had done her time while also holding down a job on *Fortune* magazine, which *Fortune* sort of expected back in those days, with left-wing intellectual wheeler-dealers like Dwight MacDonald on the staff. Deeply interested in city planning, she had become a close friend of Lewis Mumford's through whom she had met Stonorov and Kastner. Oskar had talked her into moving to Philadelphia, where he and Alfred had established their architectural partnership in an old stable. Catherine had already won first prize for an essay on city planning in a contest sponsored by the Women's Clubs of America and had used the prize money to study public housing in Europe. Out of the material she collected on that trip had come her book.

The problem, on that Sunday night in Flourtown, as Catherine, Jeanes, and Stonorov saw it, was how to get housing in America at a price the poor could afford. Our experience with the Mackley Houses had proved that only the federal government had the resources to tackle the problem adequately. The federal government would have to undertake the job.

After Kate and I had been hauled out of our bedroom to greet these unexpected guests, Catherine Bauer sat down at our kitchen table and wrote the draft of the preamble and the major provisions of what was to become H.R. (for House Rule) 12164, "A Bill to Create a United States Housing Authority."

What was needed then, from my pragmatic point of view, was a congressman to sponsor the bill, and I suggested Henry Ellenbogen. I had met Henry, a tiny Jewish refugee lawyer from Vienna, several years earlier in Governor Pinchot's office in Harrisburg. Ellenbogen was representing striking taxicab drivers in Pittsburgh, and somehow we almost instantly became friends. In 1934, Henry had run for Congress from a district in Pittsburgh that the British would call a "rotten borough" but that we called a "Mellon district" meaning that the district was ninety percent safe for any Republican candidate cleared by the Mellon interests; 1934 was the year that it wasn't safe, and Henry had been elected.

Of all the Pennsylvania congressmen I could think of,

Henry seemed to be the one most likely to agree to be our sponsor. The next thing I knew, almost without having time to pack, I was in Oskar's ancient roadster, with Catherine, on the road to Washington. We drove through the night, had breakfast together, separated to get a little sleep, then met and tracked down Henry in his quarters at what used to be called the House Office Building, now the Cannon Office Building.

What we discovered was interesting. Henry told us that he hadn't been allowed to take his seat because he hadn't been naturalized long enough, a little detail that somehow had been overlooked all through the campaign. But the House was being run by William Bankhead, a good New Deal liberal from Alabama, and Bankhead had gotten Henry an office, his salary, and all the other perquisites. Except Henry couldn't cast a vote, much less sponsor a bill.

We had no trouble at all in selling him our idea, of course, and he began to peddle Catherine's draft around Washington, getting some of his experienced colleagues to cast it into such legal language as could be presented to Congress.

Henry finally solved his seating problem and *did* introduce H.R. 12164 on April 3, 1936, only a short while after he had been formally sworn in as a member of Congress. The bill was referred to the Committee on Banking and Currency, which wasn't very much interested in either Henry or public housing.

But pressure was building. A housing bill was introduced into the Senate by Bob Wagner at almost exactly the same time, produced in very much the same way as ours. The draft of this bill had been written by Mary Simkhovitch, former head of the Greenwich Settlement House in New York. In my opinion it was very much inferior to the Ellenbogen bill. It might have gotten housing, but it overlooked what I considered an imperative provision, a labor standard for the construction firms that would build the housing.

Dave Walsh called a public hearing before his Public Works Committee on the Wagner bill, and Catherine and I went over to testify. The only two senators at the hearing were Walsh and Wagner, with whom I then had only a speaking acquaintanceship. I started out by saying that for a labor man it was the most embarrassing experience of my life to testify against a bill that had been introduced by so great a friend of labor as Senator Wagner, but I did feel that it had some serious loopholes.

Catherine, batting her eyelashes and swinging an ankle, said pretty much the same. I don't know whether it was our testimony or not, but the bill, in that form, was withdrawn. Wagner asked Catherine to work with his executive assistant, Leon Keyserling, a young graduate of Harvard Law School. Keyserling, later chief economic adviser to President Truman, was a bulldog of a pipesmoker who had already drafted several important New Deal bills, and he and Catherine got along like dog and cat at first. Eventually, however, they arrived at an understanding and put together a Senate bill very much like our House version.

The pressures for public housing continued to mount. On the House side, we proponents were campaigning to initiate hearings on the Ellenbogen bill, which involved the basics of getting congressional action: writing or telephoning all the congressmen we knew, getting our friends to write their congressmen, persuading influential constituents in the congressmens' district to write, persuading authors, professors, ministers to take up the cause. I was one of perhaps a dozen lobbyists up on the Hill almost every day, buttonholing congressmen in the corridors, at lunch, on the street. Congressmen use their offices for working and don't like to be bothered there.

That sort of lobbying has only a certain amount of leverage for a piece of national legislation. If, in addition, you get a John Phillips, the AFL state council chief in Pennsylvania, to write a letter to each Pennsylvania congressman, the letters are read because the congressmen know that John has perhaps a hundred thousand members.

A crowning piece of support that never in my wildest dreams had I envisioned getting came from the 1935 national convention of the AFL, held that year in Atlantic City.

In labor circles, that convention is famous because it is

the one at which the controversy over industrial-versus-craft organizing exploded to the point where John L. Lewis punched William Hutcheson (Big Bill) squarely in the mouth.

I had attended the convention for a variety of duties. I was a delegate; I was doing labor background pieces for *Fortune*, and they had assigned me to help cover the convention. Franklin D. Roosevelt had appointed me to the National Advisory Council of the Federal Housing Authority (FHA), and—my final reason—I hoped to put in a good word for AFL consideration of housing.

Oskar drove Alfred Kastner and me down. Kate, Catherine Bauer, Bill Jeanes, and Lenora Kastner were driven down by a new girl whom Oskar had been seeing—he later married her—named Elizabeth Foster. She was the daughter of Frank B. Foster, who was called the "Congoleum King" because of a kind of linoleum substitute that he had invented and manufactured. No top labor leader would stay anywhere in Atlantic City except at one of the big, expensive waterfront hotels, but we put up at a tiny hotel on a back street that had a superb kosher restaurant. The Reuther boys, Walter, Victor and Roy, always used to stay there.

There were three people at the convention who would play key roles in the housing program. One was Boris Shiskin, a suave and unconventional Russian who was later to be research director of the AFL. At this point he was assistant to Florence Thorne, William Green's secretary, and a valuable behind-the-scenes operator for public housing. The second person was Warren Vinton, who later wrote *The Economic Consequences of the New Deal,* slim, articulate, and very serious, making his reputation as a political writer. The third was Edward F. McGrady, the big, jovial, outgoing Irishman who had been kidnaped by the mob back in the Elizabethton strike.

McGrady had started out his working life as a newspaper pressman in Boston. He'd been president of his pressmen's local, then of the Boston Central Labor Union, then of the Massachusetts Federation of Labor; now he was William Green's assistant. McGrady later became the number-two man in the NRA, then the first assistant secretary of labor when that post was created in 1933. (Big business finally caught on to how smart McGrady was, and David Sarnoff hired him away from labor in 1937 as vice-president for labor relations with Sarnoff's Radio Corporation of America (RCA). Ed ended up his life as a director of RCA and its subsidiary, the National Broadcasting Corporation (NBC). In short, a capitalist.)

Catherine Bauer, Boris Shiskin, and Warren Vinton worked out the wording of a housing resolution that we hoped the convention might consider. I introduced Catherine to McGrady, and Ed, naturally, took a great shine to her.

Ed, at Catherine's urging, managed to get the housing resolution on the agenda, against all the rules of the convention—resolutions were supposed to come from the resolutions committee—and in all the excitement over the fight between Lewis and Hutcheson, it went unnoticed. The excitement was so intense, also, that there wasn't even any debate on the resolution.

It simply passed.

After all our planning and preparations, what transpired seemed almost an anticlimax, but now we had the AFL behind us. When the AFL speaks, Congress listens. Pressures for public housing began to rise on all sides. Building-trades unions around the country began to realize that it would mean more jobs; building-materials manufacturers from steel to paint began to realize that it would mean more sales. The old arguments that it was visionary and socialistic began to dwindle.

Almost immediately after the AFL convention, Catherine moved to Washington, got herself some respectable clothes—probably against her better instincts, because up to then she'd always dressed like a Greenwich Village ragamuffin—and snuggled up to the building-trades boys. And those old goats, always to a man opposed to public housing and to women's rights, to a man they fell in love with her. They set up a budget to help her work on housing, introduced her around, and helped her to establish an organization called the Labor

Housing Conference, later the National Labor Housing Conference.

One facet of getting effective social legislation passed is that so many factors are involved, so many varied interests, and so many human vagaries. I would estimate that the original Wagner-Ellenbogen housing bill was rewritten twenty times; when it was finally passed—because of this human factor—Henry's name wasn't even on it.

In the beginning, Franklin Roosevelt was of no help to us at all. Even when he began to support housing, it wasn't for housing's sake, but because nearly a third of the nation's unemployed were in the building trades. He knew that, one way or another, he simply had to lick the unemployment problem to avoid anarchy in the country. In 1934, the passage of the National Housing Act created the FHA. All that did was to give a federal guarantee to loans for people who already had sufficient assets to borrow the money in the first place. Moreover, Roosevelt appointed James Moffett to head up the agency. Moffett may have been a fine man for all I know, but he was president of Standard Oil of New Jersey, and he was on record as opposed to the whole concept of the FHA. The FHA, Moffett said, would "wreck the whole twenty-one-billion-dollar mortgage market." We began to refer to the FHA as the "F—— Housing Altogether" agency.

Then two things happened. Roosevelt saw, despite caring little about public housing, that it had become so important an issue that he had to put his weight behind it. And Henry Steagall, chairman of the House Banking and Currency Committee—an old s.o.b. if there ever was one, absolutely opposed to the bill from the word go—finally said he'd report it out if it had his name on it.

That's how you get legislation passed. Steagall, in the climate of the times, saw a chance to become an overnight liberal. His committee reported the bill out, the House passed it, and finally, on September 1, 1937, Roosevelt signed the Wagner-Steagall Housing Act that created the United States Housing Authority (USHA).

One of the features of the final act was that it provided for the creation of local housing authorities. The federal government was not going to march in, like Orwell's Big Brother, and decree where public housing was needed and therefore where it would be built. The federal government would supply the money and set certain standards, but the local communities would control the sites of the projects.

The National Housing Conference (NHC) was established, a citizens' bipartisan coalition of which I was named a member.

In retrospect, I believe that the final triumph for public housing was the War Housing Act passed in 1942, and simply because it was passed virtually without debate.

No running around chasing after congressmen, no night drives to Washington or Atlantic City, no arguments about whether it represented the opening wedge of socialism. It simply was passed. Public housing had become an accepted concept. After fifteen years of lobbying for this dream, what made me the happiest was that nobody at all paid any attention to it—an even greater honor than the greatly appreciated citation given me at the Statler-Hilton Hotel in Washington in February 1963 by the NHC.

That part of housing is past and done. Today, I must say that I agree with those critics who point out that there was a major flaw in the way the housing program was carried out: the leveling of slums and the erecting of mammoth cold brick and concrete thirty- and forty-story skyscrapers. By thinking only of buildings, the planners entirely forgot the human element. The Carl Mackley Houses were right in their concept: four stories high, plenty of grass and trees, room for children to play, a complete social fabric planned. Today, too many of the housing projects we fought so hard for are in their turn becoming slums. I recognize the problems inherent in designing projects for six hundred families rather than one hundred (as in Carl Mackley) and in the skyrocketing cost of land, labor, and construction materials. But the fact remains that when the buildings take over, the human quality is destroyed.

I am not overly discouraged; the concept of providing housing exists, and today's planners, or at least the good ones both here and abroad, are turning to a pluralistic approach to housing. By that they are trying to rehabilitate neighborhoods —the best of the old—worth saving. When they build new housing, they more often are using the "new cities" formula, which concerns itself not simply with buildings but with the whole human way of living.

Chapter Nine

I SHOULD THANK old Sam Gompers for my first trip abroad as an adult, in 1936. He had always wanted the AFL to take part in the international labor movement and to become a participating member of the International Labor Organization (ILO), originally set up by the League of Nations. Nothing had come of it at the time, nor for fifteen years afterward until, during Roosevelt's first term, the State Department under Cordell Hull began to try to re-establish some neglected international relationships. One was with foreign labor, and the first official American delegation to the ILO was sent over in 1935.

Frances Perkins was pretty angry at the AFL for its performance in picking the delegation, for which I don't blame her in the least. The bumbling leaders of the old guard (they called themselves "international" presidents, which generally meant that they had one local in Canada) saw no reason at all to concern themselves with the problems of labor abroad, and not a single "international" president was a member of the American delegation.

The 1936 delegation, to which I was named, was slightly different, even though, again, not one top AFL official was a member. The delegation was headed by John G. Winant, former governor of New Hampshire and a close friend of Roosevelt's. (Roosevelt later named him chairman of the Social Security Board, then ambassador to the Court of St. James's.)

During the early months of 1936, I spent almost all of my time in the field. Returning to our spanking new offices in Philadelphia in April, I was completely bowled over when Rieve informed me that he had accepted an invitation from the State Department to be an American delegate and that he wanted me to go to Europe with him as his official adviser. Much as I relished the idea of the trip, I was not thrilled.

"There's too much to do here, Emil," I remember telling him. "The whole climate is ripe for organizing, and we shouldn't be traipsing over to Europe."

But the temptation of going there as an official American delegate was too much for Rieve.

"If you don't want to go," he said, "I'll tell the State Department that I can't go, either."

Despite my conviction that we should both stay in the United States and attend to union affairs, I basically did want to go, too, so it wasn't a hard decision for me to make. (But I was still so involved with union problems that I almost missed the boat—literally—because I had forgotten to obtain a French visa for my passport. I had to leave Kate and the children, who had come to see me off, at the pier while I took a cab to the office of the French consul general in New York to get the required stamp.)

The trip across was a wonderful holiday for me—in fact, I suddenly realized how long I'd been working hard, and I felt as if I were on a spree. All we really had to do every day on the crossing was to attend an afternoon briefing session, by one of the Labor Department crew of experts who accompanied us, on the issues to be brought up at the conference. Two other members of the delegation I got to know quite well were Marion Hedges, the ebullient, rotund research director for the Electrical Workers (and editor of its monthly journal), and J. C. Lewis, a UMW official and president of the Iowa State Federation of Labor.

We spent three days in Paris, living in a modest hotel on the Left Bank, eating in inexpensive (but stunningly good) restaurants, and seeing sights (besides the standard tourist treks) presumed to be of special interest to labor skates, such as the Renault plant on the outskirts of the city.

In Geneva we found ourselves put up in a hotel a good deal fancier than expected and had our first experience in truly international dealings. I for one had never before seen in operation either simultaneous translation or any of the other techniques for dealing with multilanguage conferences that have now become so familiar. Nor had I ever been at a labor conference at which some of the delegates wore turbans and long flowing robes. Our briefing officer in Geneva was a handsome young stripling, a State Department career officer named Charles Bohlen, later ambassador to Russia.

Socially, it was a wonderful time, for the ILO had organized sightseeing trips on boats around Lake Geneva and on buses into the Alps.

The formal sessions were incredibly dull, even when they were addressed by orators as powerful and labor leaders as distinguished as the French socialist giant Leon Jouhaux, the leader of the Confédération Génerale du Travail from 1909 to 1947, when he resigned because of its alliance with the communists. (He went on to help found the International Confederation of Free Trade Unions and, in 1951, won the Nobel Peace Prize.)

The caucuses of the separate groups of delegates were far more interesting. It was here that the Russian delegates argued interminably about the decadence of all Western trade unions, that the sole function of the trade union was to represent the interests of the workers in the councils of the people. The Spanish delegates made truly moving speeches (the Republican government was still in power at this time) about the ruthless oppression of the fascists and the equally ruthless assaults of the communists.

The principal item on the agenda, as far as Rieve and I were concerned, was one proposing a worldwide minimum wage for the textile industry. It kept me busy writing speeches for Rieve for a full ten days trying to explain the basic fact that a minimum wage that would cause dancing in the streets in India would cause a general strike in England or the United States.

When the conference ended in Geneva, Rieve went off on a quick Cook's tour of Italy while Hedges and I went to London; then I was able to see my mother and sister for the first time in years. I also went to visit my uncle, John Steele, for which I'm grateful; as it turned out, though he lived for quite a number of years after that, it was the last time I was to see him.

Rieve finally joined Hedges and me in London, and besides the usual sightseeing for which I was proud to be the conductor, we sat in on an international socialist conference and a meeting of the British trade unions, where we saw Ernest Bevin in action.

There was a subtle advantage that accrued to the United States, not so much from this particular international conference as from the United States's reappearance on the international scene. It did not become apparent until a few years later when, early in World War II, England and America suddenly realized that loyal trade-union members in occupied Europe were among the most effective saboteurs and agents against the Nazis. My sister Sonia was one of those recruited by Allen Dulles, then one of the top operators for the Office of Strategic Services, to set up the liaison with the Europeans she knew. I like to think that ILO conference in Geneva helped to pave the way.

My bonds with Rieve had gone back almost to my earliest days in the Hosiery Workers, but this trip strengthened them immeasurably.

When I had first moved to Philadelphia, the president of the Hosiery branch there (the union's biggest) had been a fine man named Gustave Geiges, who later quit the union to become a mill manager. To replace Geiges, the executive board of the union had submitted two names for election: Carl Holderman of Paterson, New Jersey (who later was to become a good friend of mine), and Rieve, from Milwaukee, a Pole by birth, who had been a "footer" in his mill and was a rising young official in the union. Rieve's parents had brought him to this country when he was a child of four or five, but for some reason he spoke English with a pronounced Polish accent all his life. I had met him a number of times when he had come to Philadelphia to attend the quarterly board meetings, and we had formed a bond because I found that he liked to go to concerts and plays as often as I. Most of the other board members liked to play cards in their hotel rooms or go out on the town.

I did not know Holderman well at that time, but even then I was firmly convinced that Rieve was the better man to lead the union. I still am. For one thing, beyond being a highly skilled worker, which carried its own prestige in Hosiery, Rieve was known throughout the union. He had worked in Milwaukee, Philadelphia, New Jersey, and Indiana. Despite his accent he was an effective speaker. He performed especially well in the rough-and-tumble debate of union meetings. In addition, he was one of the shrewdest and most skilled negotiators in the entire AFL—as he proved later when he became president of the Textile Workers—and he developed very rapidly into an efficient administrator. He was so good, in fact, that the Hosiery Workers, though subordinate to the Textile Workers, became known as one of the most important unions in the AFL.

Throughout the years, my only trouble with Rieve was from the publicity point of view. Even later, when he became an important figure not only in the labor movement but in political and governmental circles in Washington and New York, he adamantly refused to step into the limelight or to go out of his way, outside the labor movement, to cultivate men who would have been useful. I must confess I have the same temperament myself, but while that is all right for someone who was in my position, a president of a union loses something of his effectiveness by being so retiring.

When Rieve and I returned from the ILO meeting in the late summer of 1936, the labor atmosphere around Philadelphia had changed radically. The new organizing drives were being initiated.

The fatal flaw of the old AFL leadership, as I have said, was that it did not recognize that there were masses of industrial workers simply waiting to be organized. A typical example of its failure was its halfhearted attempt to organize the automobile workers in 1934. It went into the auto plants as if attempting to organize a printing plant. Printing is a skilled profession, and if you organize printers, you have the industry organized. In the automobile industry, however, skilled workers are in a minority. You can train anyone to be an assembly-line worker in a few weeks.

The outstanding opponents of this method of organizing within labor were those AFL unions that either had nothing to lose or much to gain by an industrial system of organization. A John L. Lewis, for example, would not be risking anything by the industrial organization of the steel industry, for if steel could be organized, the UMW stood to gain. Neither Dave Dubinsky of the ILGWU nor Sidney Hillman of the Amalgamated Clothing Workers (ACW) risked anything. (They had also been at odds with the rest of the AFL leadership for years.) The Radio and Machine Workers, which had organized the big Philco plant in Philadelphia, had everything to gain; Emil Rieve of the Hosiery Workers had nothing to lose.

Toward the end of the summer of 1936, the pro-industrial-organizational unions in Philadelphia formed what they called the Committee for Industrial Organization of the City of Philadelphia. They managed to scrape up two or three thousand dollars to start an organizing drive.

Rieve asked me to leave Hosiery and take command of this operation. One of the founding fathers of the CIO and named head of the Philadelphia committee, Rieve told me, "John, it is your duty to the trade union movement to take this job."

It was not an easy decision for me to make. I had a good, solid job at Hosiery and a future in a union that I very much liked and admired. Strange how little things influence you, too. I didn't want to leave my beautiful, spacious, glass-walled office in the new union headquarters that Oskar Stonorov had remodeled for the union on North Broad Street right near the new Reading Railroad station in North Philadelphia; it was so easy to hop a train for my home in Flourtown.

And I *liked* being research director for the Hosiery Workers, editing the *Hosiery Worker,* and lobbying.

Joining the CIO meant moving to an amorphous organization that had no guarantee even of its very existence. There was no salary inducement; that would still be seventy-five dollars a week. But I firmly believed that the future of labor lay in industrial organization. If I passed up this opportunity, I would regret it all my life. I might never get one like it again.

When Rieve finished talking to me, even though I told him I needed time to think it over, I knew that I would take it. I went home and told Kate, and she, as I knew she would, agreed.

Thus, I left Hosiery, after thirteen rewarding years, to join what was to become the CIO (the Congress of Industrial Organizations) as we know it today. (Though the initials were the same, what I originally joined was the Committee for Industrial Organization.)

I harbored one doubt, however. I was not really a professional labor organizer—which, in the early thirties, was becoming an increasingly more skilled and complicated profession. To be a topnotch professional organizer, you had to be a good speaker, and you had to have a mind for facts and figures, an endless supply of physical energy, and a willingness to accept the brutal fact that you could end up in a hospital ward after a beating at the hands of the police or of management thugs.

Before I had been confronted by any such tests, however—in fact, barely after I had set up a tiny grimy office in Philadelphia with a secretary and one paid organizer under my command—the annual convention of the AFL was held in Atlantic City in October 1936.

Without a doubt, it was the most important labor convention of the century, the one at which John L. Lewis had determined to force the federation onto the path of industrial organization or pull the miners out of the AFL and start a new organization of his own.

Lewis himself, despite his deficiencies—the principal public one, a strange political blindness; the personal one, overweening arrogance—was one of the two or three greatest labor leaders of the century. He possessed three qualities necessary for greatness in any field. He was smart, he was tough, and he was lucky. Hillman may have been as smart, and Dubinsky may have been as tough, but neither of them had the luck to lead a union that was absolutely essential to the economy of the nation. If the clothing workers or the garment workers went out on strike, it might mean that men might have to wear the same old suit for another six months, or women the same old dress. But if the miners went out on strike, it meant that there would be no fuel for heat, power, or electricity.

Lewis came into the 1936 AFL convention armed for bear—meaning the AFL top leadership. His particular target was the AFL's anti-industrial-union stance, and his particular weapon was a resolution he proposed that craft unions were to have no craft jurisdiction over workers organized in mass-production industries.

The resolution was defeated.

The day after the convention ended, Lewis held a conference in his suite at the Hotel President to draft plans for the CIO. Also present were Hillman and Dubinsky; two of his closest aides: John Brophy, who had been a major force in the UMW, and that charming old Scotsman, Philip Murray, master of intricacy, who was later to succeed Lewis as president of the CIO; the aging president of the UTWU, Thomas W. McMahon; the tall and sharp-faced president of the International Typographical Union, Charles P. Howard; Max Zaritsky, then head of the Cap and Millinery Department of the United Hatters Union; and Thomas J. Kennedy, Lewis's former number-one associate, secretary-treasurer of the UMW, and head of its anthracite division (always the base of Lewis's power), now lieutenant governor of Pennsylvania and an old friend of mine—I had been his primary campaign manager.

On November 23, 1936, Lewis wrote his famous fourteen-word letter to William Green. "Dear Sir and Brother," he wrote. "Effective this date, I resign as vice-president of the American Federation of Labor."

So, the break had been made.

It was inevitable. God knows that the jurisdictional disputes in the AFL were themselves serious enough—and still are—but they are rather theological—such as how many angels can dance on the head of a pin. Important to those involved in them, but nothing more. The greater role of labor lay in mass organization, in improving the standard of living of the average worker, rather than in endless disputes over whether the operating engineer or the hoist operator should do such and such a job or how many electricians should be required backstage at a Theater Guild production.

I was under no great illusion as to why I had been chosen to head up organizing for the Philadelphia committee. Despite my lack of experience in organizing, I was well enough known in labor circles in Pennsylvania and New Jersey that my name would mean something in the newspapers.

After I made my decision to go with the committee, I really had no specific idea of what I was going to do first, but I needn't have worried. From the very first hours in my shabby new office, literally before I had been able to get an oblong of clean blotting paper for the top of my desk or to find some notepads, an almost steady stream of people began to visit me. Many of them were ordinary working people who had read or heard about the new organizing drive. It was an extraordinary experience for me. In some of the Hosiery organizing drives in which I had been involved, after we had set up a headquarters and persuaded, cajoled, made speeches, canvassed house to house, gotten publicity—yes, then we had had people come in off the street and sign with the union. But simply to have people come in off the street and say that they worked at such and such a plant and wanted to join the union was a wholly new experience.

Of course, most of them didn't have the faintest notion of what joining a union meant. They thought that if they joined and we gave them a membership card, all their problems would be solved automatically. Their grievances against the company, whatever they were, would magically vanish the next day, their wages would go up, they would have no more worries.

That we had no instant solutions, that we would have to get a majority of their fellow workers to sign up, that we would have to have collective-bargaining-agent elections, that we would collect dues, that they would have to go to union meetings—all the operating mechanism of a union meant very little to them.

One incident from those days illustrates my point. We organized a small mattress-manufacturing plant at which the going wage was twenty-five cents an hour, and we were in the process of negotiating a contract with the management that would have doubled the rate. One of the new union members came into my office and, after a good deal of hemming and hawing, expressed doubt that the union was giving him a fair shake. He operated one of the machines that filled the mattresses and therefore made two cents an hour more than the basic wage. He agreed that doubling his pay appealed to him, but he felt that his differential should also be doubled (for we had retained the two-cents-an-hour differential). He finally agreed to let us take up his complaint *after* we had signed a contract—the plant's first labor contract.

For all my prejudices and convictions, I must admit that the Communist Party was of help to me in the early organizing days.

To my mind the clear distinction between the communist and the socialist is that the socialist believes in both the political and economic rights of man; with the communist, political rights stop at the Party door. Without hesitation I could name a half-dozen socialist governments that tolerate communist parties; there is no communist government that tolerates any political party except its own.

For the very reason of its totalitarian "the-government-knows-all-is-all-seeing-and-all-wise" ideology, communism has a great appeal for the impatient and superficial mind. My friend Louis Budenz turned to communism (and eventually, because he was too tolerant for them, turned back).

More in the Philadelphia area than anywhere else in the country in those days, not even excepting the New York area, the Communist Party was moving into the organizational vacuum that the AFL had abdicated and the CIO had not yet filled. Real sweatshop conditions did exist; wage levels were so low as to defy comprehension today. To cite only one instance: in 1933 in Philadelphia, women workers in the paper-bag industry started at three dollars a week for a fifty-two-hour work week, men started at six dollars, and broken bags were deducted from their wages.

Capitalizing on the misery and frustration inherent in such situations, the communists had already begun to recruit sweatshop workers into the Party, and they were quick to see that the new CIO, as a useful and respectable organization, might serve their ends.

I first began to notice what the communists were doing by the number of people who came to my office for advice on organizing sent there by the communists—either openly communist organizations or those that used the most transparent of euphemisms. (To this day, when I hear the head of a communist state describe himself as the leader of a "people's republic," I get the same feeling I used to get back when Hitler was describing himself as leader of a "socialist workers' republic.")

I was faced with a real dilemma. I was fully aware of the dangers of allowing the communists a foot in the door. I also knew that if I could not mount a real organizing drive, and quickly, I would be missing my chance. I had a pitiful amount of money, no organization, and a staff of one besides myself.

I was, in short, in no position to turn down whatever help I could get from the communists.

I therefore decided on two courses of action.

In the first place, I knew the district organizer for the Communist Party fairly well—Patrick John Tuohy, a big, handsome, black-haired, hard-working, affable, dedicated man. If he had not been so wedded to the Communist Party, we might have become quite good friends; even to the end of his life we exchanged Christmas cards.

I called Pat up, and we met, just the two of us. Each knew where the other stood, and there was no fencing necessary—or almost none. I told Pat that I needed as much help as I could get but that I was not at all prepared to see any plants that I could organize turned into cells for the Communist Party. If he really believed in the welfare of the workers, I said, he would help me all he could.

Now I probably knew the general orders under which Pat was operating as well as he. After all, I could read the *Daily Worker*, which faithfully printed the American party line, dictated daily from Moscow.

I think that Pat and I arrived at a meeting of the minds. I knew that he was convinced that the organizing he and his people could do would ultimately redound to the credit of the Party—American communists in those days really did believe in the ultimate collapse of American capitalism. I, however, was absolutely determined that Pat was not going to use the CIO as a cover for his own drive, especially in my own headquarters. In the end, we more or less agreed on this sort of stand-off.

The second major step I took to get my organizing drive under way was to fall back on my old socialist connections and recruit their help.

From the Young People's Socialist League, I was able to get the unpaid but dedicated and full-time services of three young men—Harold Ash, Murray Kimmelman, and Sidney Schulman—all just graduated from Temple University and all from families who provided them food and shelter after they had finished their work—an important consideration in those days, as it was weeks before I could even scrape up enough to pay them carfare and lunch money. But they were able, energetic, and dedicated.

I also began to recruit volunteers from among my students at the workers' education courses I had conducted while working for Branch One of the Hosiery Workers. Other organizers I got were simply jobless workers who saw that there was a task to be accomplished and who wanted to help.

One volunteer I got just walked in off the street, a Canadian citizen of Greek origin named George Charles, later a valued personal and family friend. Charles had been chef on a merchant ship but had quit to spend a few months visiting a married sister in Philadelphia; he had then decided that he wanted a job. Being a good union man—a member of the Maritime Union—he came to me. He was a tall and strong young man—both valuable assets in a union organizer in those days—and he also had a natural charm that made him one of my best workers. (Later, after an outstanding career in the US Army in World War II, he studied law, for some time was counsel for the Greek Embassy in Washington, and is now in private law practice.)

It was at this point that John L. Lewis, his split with the AFL now an accomplished fact, took command of the national organizing campaign of the CIO.

The first contact that I had ever had with Lewis was in the late summer of 1934 when I was Philadelphia manager for the primary campaign for lieutenant governor of Thomas J. Kennedy, the big, smooth Irishman who was one of Lewis's closest associates. I had known Kennedy as a friend of my old mentor, Jim Maurer, and because we had both been equally involved in state politics.

Lewis had taken a very close personal interest in Kennedy's campaign, and since Philadelphia was one of the key areas that labor had to carry, Lewis was constantly on the phone from his office in Washington. (We won.)

For all the times that I saw Lewis and talked to him, I'm not sure that even today I completely understand him. On the one hand, he was the driving force in establishing industrial unionism in the United States—which would seem to classify him as a "liberal" labor leader. At the same time he was a vociferous isolationist in foreign affairs. This is a contradiction that I cannot explain. Many of our equally "liberal" men in domestic affairs—Senators William Borah and George Norris, to name only two—were equally isolationist in foreign matters.

One reason may be that isolationism, beyond its traditional attraction, had been given a great deal of impetus in this country in the thirties—especially among labor leaders and liberals in general—by the Senate hearings conducted by North Dakota's Gerald P. Nye into the American government's military loans in World War I. The hearings left the distinct impression that the sole reason for World War I was to enrich the manufacturers of munitions and that the United States government and the "international bankers" had financed it. The hearings also eventually (in 1935) resulted in the passage of the Neutrality Act that was to cause so much trouble for Roosevelt later.

It may be that I don't "understand" Lewis because I have no evidence that he understood himself. He aspired to great things. He achieved great things. Did he really dream of becoming president? I don't know. I certainly never talked to him about it, but if the thought ever did cross his mind, he must have known at once that such an ambition could never be realized—though I have never known a man to be a total realist with himself. A man of Lewis's gifts, able to forge the UMW into the most powerful union in the country, able to defeat the very real threat of communists taking over his union, able to defy the powers of the United States Senate (able to out-think and to out-talk a whole series of Senate committees), and able to defy the president of the United States—what did he dream beyond all that? It is no wonder, I think, that as the years passed, Lewis became increasingly tyrannical, increasingly domineering, increasingly withdrawn.

In any event, Lewis took over the national organizing drive of the CIO, and the man he put in charge was John Brophy. Brophy's appointment was yet another evidence of the complexity of Lewis's character. In 1926, when the American mining industry was nothing less than a disaster area because of the vast overproduction of bituminous coal, Brophy had run against Lewis for the presidency of the UMW. Brophy thought that Lewis's hard-line policy of maintaining the core of relatively highly paid anthracite workers as the basis of the union was wrong. I'm sure that Lewis looked on Brophy's candidacy not as a theoretical difference over strategy but as a personally motivated assault on his own seat of power.

Brophy lost, and Lewis did everything but throw him out of the union. He would have done that too, had it been possible. While Lewis had little loyalty to anyone except his very closest associates, he demanded unquestioning subservience from everyone around him. Challenging his authority was, in his eyes, as egregious a fault as peculation of union funds.

Lewis, however, never let his personal feelings stand in the way of what he wanted done, and he knew that Brophy was a topnotch labor organizer and (mostly, I think, because Brophy was a devout Catholic) as anticommunist as Lewis himself. Lewis, astute as ever, recognized the communist threat to the new labor organization long before any of his critics.

When Lewis needed Brophy, therefore, he decided to let bygones be bygones and appointed Brophy as one of his chief lieutenants.

When Brophy took over the organizing drive, he inherited a whole squad of Lewis's assistants, and he quickly recognized that they were nothing but old-time mine union hacks very much set on doing things in the good old way. They would be of almost no use whatsoever in a totally new situation. To help me in my organizing drive, Brophy sent me four such men. I told him that simply wasn't going to work out.

We both knew what Lewis was doing. He was spending vast amounts of money on the CIO organizing drive out of the UMW treasury, and, as a practical man, he had to employ mine workers in that drive. He had to provide jobs for them; it was that simple. Most of them were good, loyal mine unionists, but they were fish out of water in a variegated urban-industrial district like eastern Pennsylvania. The Philadelphia area had no dominant industry. The textile industry was the biggest, but there was an almost endless list of others: the Philco radio plant, the Philadelphia Gas Company, distilleries, wineries. The helpers I got had no understanding of trade practices in these industries, no knowledge of wage levels, no established patterns for organizing them.

I told Brophy that I intended to rely principally on my young socialist people—and myself—for the real organizing work, and he agreed. He took back his people, and never again was I interfered with from the Washington headquarters on that particular phase of the drive.

Looking back, I see that I was now entering a period of the most intensive work of my life. I say that as a man who was no stranger to hard work—who liked it, in fact. I wouldn't know what to do with myself if I couldn't work. But—through all my years at Hosiery, for example—I was part of a going organization. If I needed help, I could get it. Here, I had no one. I had my young socialists, who were dedicated and tireless workers without experience, and, briefly, my old mine workers, who were not tireless, but whose experience was in a totally different field.

I would get to my office at seven o'clock, hoping to get through my paperwork, only to find two or three people waiting for me. I don't think I had a regular lunch, one where I really sat down at a table with food put in front of me, more than a couple of times a month. The rest of the time I ate, at my desk or at somebody else's, sandwiches and coffee in paper containers, talking business. And the telephone! I'd hate to try to work out the number of hours—or years—that I've spent on the telephone. In the evenings we had meetings, sometimes as many as six or eight going on at the same time in the innumerable rooms of our old building. I'd go from one to the next, giving a short speech at each.

That I never begrudged a moment of such hard work was because I felt it to be the most important job that I could possibly hope to do, ever. It was, if you will, a crusade. I know my wife understood that—what other wife would put up with the sort of life she led?—and somehow she communicated it to the children. Many years later, my elder daughter Alison, asked how she had felt about seeing her father for a total of perhaps eight hours a week, said, "We always felt as if he were a soldier in the front-line trenches."

I wouldn't have put it quite so dramatically myself, but nonetheless there was a revolutionary atmosphere in those days.

To re-emphasize, my sheer lack of help was by all odds my most severe handicap. Besides the industries I have already mentioned, we were also simultaneously attempting to organize a Bethlehem Steel Company plant, a couple of oil refineries, agricultural workers, two or three highly specialized plants making surgical knives and other expensive medical equipment, graveyard workers, the Campbell Soup plant at Camden, chemical and drug plants, the Sun shipyards (at Camden, New Jersey), steel fabricators, the huge Viscose plant (owned by the British munitions maker Vicker) at Marcus Hook, and so on.

I traded shamelessly on my own personal connections, however fragile.

I remember a sit-down strike that took place in the big Dixie Cup Company manufacturing plant. Sit-down strikes were getting to be a familiar form of labor demonstration in those days. We had not yet held a National Labor Relations Board (NLRB) election in the plant, so we were not legally authorized to speak for the employees.

The president of Dixie Cup was a great Bach fan and a major contributor to the annual Bach festival that had long been a traditional cultural event at Bethlehem, Pennsylvania. I knew that, and somewhere along the line he had heard that I too was a great Bach fan who also used to attend the festivals. Thus I was able to get him to agree to see me in his office at his main plant in Easton. He and I spent almost the entire afternoon talking about Bach and the role of music in life.

Finally, we discussed the sit-in strike. By that time we had so complete a meeting of the minds that he agreed almost in a couple of sentences to permit an NLRB election.

Then the workers wouldn't believe the company statement, and when the NLRB representative arrived, he and I had to use a stepladder to climb the wire fence outside the plant to persuade the employees that the company had indeed made the agreement.

One of our most successful early organizing drives in Philadelphia involved the hotel industry. Before the Depression, the AFL Hotel and Restaurant Workers had established a solid local in Philadelphia, but the Depression had just about ruined the hotel business; a great many of the major hotels in my district—not to mention elsewhere in the country—were in receivership. In addition, particularly in the Philadelphia–New York area, the communists had moved in. In Philadelphia this had led to vicious infighting within the union. Contractual relationships between the shaky hotel managements and the feud-ridden union local were utterly worthless when the CIO arrived on the scene. Hotel employees were working almost under conditions of serfdom. Most of the hotels had given up anything except token gestures at maintenance: radiators gave no heat, burned-out light bulbs were not replaced, cockroaches were taking over the kitchens.

Organizing the hotel workers was in some ways a pleasure for me, largely because the cooks and waiters were such a volatile lot, and so cosmopolitan that the average union meeting was a babble of languages—French, German, Hungarian, Italian, English—as they all translated for each other.

It was also an enlightening experience. I had never realized that the hotel business was such a day-to-day affair as far as employees went. If a hotel were going to have a banquet, it would need an extra hundred waiters—but only for that banquet. If it booked in three hundred guests for a convention, it would need an extra twenty maids—but only for that week. It was my first real experience with what is called casual employment.

A nice incident remains in my mind as a footnote to the hotel workers' organizing drive. A few months later a strike took place in an old established tannery in Tioga County in northern Pennsylvania. We were finally able to get agreement to hold a conference in Philadelphia at which both sides would try to work out their differences. The representative for the tannery was a state senator and a major political figure throughout the state.

The conference, held in the grand old Bellevue–Stratford Hotel in the center of Philadelphia, broke up just after midnight, and I accompanied the senator to his suite to try to make a couple of points that I thought hadn't been covered clearly enough during the conference. The senator was tired; although agreeing to listen to me, he wanted a drink. He rang for room service, and when the waiter arrived and the senator had ordered for himself—I don't drink—the waiter said: "You know, Senator, it's after midnight, and the law says that I can't serve you a drink." Then the waiter looked at me and continued, "But I see that there sits Mr. Edelman, the head of the CIO hereabouts, and if he says it's okay, then I'll bring up a drink for you."

We were successful in organizing the hotel workers, which had two further results. On the one hand, it led to an even greater influx of workers who wanted to be organized, and on the other, it led to even more intensive efforts by the employers to keep us out. Newspaper campaigns were launched against us, charging the CIO as nothing but an arm of the Communist Party; our dues levies, they stated, were a systematic attempt to rob the worker of money that lawfully belonged to him.

My work in those days was so frantic that I shall simply mention some of the things I was doing:

- Philadelphia Transit. The Philadelphia Transit Company had its own union, which was pretty ineffectual in accomplishing anything for the workers. Mike Quill (Michael Joseph) in New York City was in the process of establishing what was to become the Transport Workers Union, with the help, again, of the indefatigable Communist Party. He was very much interested in organizing the transit workers in Philadelphia. He was building his New York union on the basis of a moribund company union, and he saw no reason why he couldn't accomplish the same ninety miles south. The Philadelphia local leaders were, of course, frightened to death of Quill. But Quill and I had something in common, based on my youthful admiration for James Larkin, the radical socialist Irish labor leader who had founded the Irish Transport and General Workers Union. For years (as I've mentioned), one of my treasured possessions was a red lapel button in the shape of a hand, the symbol of the Irish Transport Workers, given me by Larkin. Quill was an admirer of Larkin, too, and the first thing he spotted at our first meeting was the red lapel button that I had made a point of wearing. Through this bond with Quill, and out of my own personal acquaintance with the leadership of the Philadelphia company union, I was able to set up the first of the meetings that led to the formation of the Philadelphia Transport Workers Union.

• We had a vast white-collar operation. I had deliberately stayed pretty well away from organizing the American Newspaper Guild in eastern Pennsylvania, feeling that if newspapermen themselves didn't have the wit and drive to form their own union, that was their affair. But since I knew the publisher of the *Tribune*, the morning newspaper in Reading, so well, I did help negotiate the contract at that paper and got the guild its first union-shop, dues-checkoff contract in the country. I was able to achieve one other accomplishment in the white-collar field for the employees of the state relief agency, the Department of Public Assistance. One of the first grievances I found lay in the standards of the Civil Service examinations. Not for an instant did anyone dream of returning to the old spoils system of appointing and promoting state employees, but the examinations were so completely geared to the level of formal schooling that many able and intelligent people either couldn't get a job or couldn't get promoted. My own lack of formal education made me particularly sensitive to this. An old Philadelphia Quaker banker was head of the state committee that set hiring standards for civil service employees. I got him to come to Flourtown one Sunday afternoon, and in a period of a few hours he agreed to recommend a new system of examination for employees in which oral examinations would complement written tests. Not only did this solution—which was adopted—provide an answer to one of the major grievances of the welfare workers, it was so successful that I cannot see why it is not adopted for Civil Service employees at every level of government—local, state, and federal. I spent several days at Harrisburg serving with a five-man board which had been appointed to select non-appointive employees under the new system, and I was surprised to find how often the board, which included three hardheaded businessmen, was unanimous in agreeing on the chosen candidate.

Those days, too, were punctuated with violence.

My own most tension-filled experience in the entire organizing campaign—the one in which I was dead sure, for a couple of hours, that I was done for—occurred at the Hershey Chocolate company plant in the town of Hershey, which is quite close to Harrisburg. The Hershey company was very paternalistic and had built the town to house the company's employees in a "model" village. Milton Hershey, the company founder who died at Hershey in 1945, was generous in many ways; he had donated sixty million dollars to found the Hershey Industrial School for orphan boys. Despite his personal philanthropies and despite the "model" aspects of the town, with its own hotel and recreation centers, schools, and fire and police departments, by 1937 the workers in the Hershey factories had decided that they wanted more of a voice in their own affairs.

About one thousand men and women workers staged a sitdown strike to force the company to allow them to form a union. We at the CIO in Philadelphia had been talking about trying to organize Hershey for months, but every time we had sent an organizer to the town, he had been run out by the company police.

With the sit-down strike, however, a new element had entered the situation. After a few days of idleness, the factory had begun to notify the local dairy farmers, who made their livelihood by selling their milk and cream to Hershey, that their supplies would not be needed for the duration of the sit-down.

Hershey management officials, as we later proved at NLRB hearings, under the direct orders of old Mr. Hershey himself, also began to hold meetings with the farmers, telling them that if they wanted to start selling dairy products again, the best way to do so was to break the strike. The farmers began to gather outside the mill every day intent on beating up anyone they could find who was supporting the sit-in.

The Hershey strike began to get headlines in newspapers all over the East. (Many papers represented the "embattled" farmers as heroes defending "the American way" against the "communistic" factory workers who had taken over private property.) It was at this point that I decided to investigate for myself the situation at Hershey.

I was becoming pretty well known in Pennsylvania in those days because the newspapers, particularly in Philadelphia and Harrisburg, were beginning to pay more and more attention to labor, strikes, and organizing drives and, to a lesser extent, to my role in them. So in Hershey I was greeted by the authorities with a kind of controlled hostility, but I received permission to call a meeting in a field near the Hershey plant. It turned out to be a small meeting—only a handful of the strikers dared show up—but I was surprised to see present quite a number of farm hands, not the farm operators—though some of them came, mostly out of curiosity as to what I had to say—but Italian immigrants who had been recruited to work on the farms from the nearby cities. I tried to explain that the farm workers and the factory workers had mutual interests, that they were both victims of the Hershey system. While the factory workers were subject directly to the Hershey law of wages, jobs, and even to whether they had a job at all, the farm workers were also subject to it, for where else could the milk from the farms be sold except to Hershey? Hershey was the only commercial buyer. I think that drew a generally favorable response, but in concrete terms I was not able to accomplish anything, and I returned to Philadelphia feeling frustrated.

A few days later, a rare gem of a woman entered my office to volunteer to work for me. She was Mrs. Mary Schneider, widow of one of the first city managers in the United States, an elderly and aristocratic-appearing woman with a small income of her own. She also had a law degree and simply wanted to work for a good cause. She had a remarkable presence. She dressed primly, spoke softly and feared nothing. No matter how explosive the situation, she always acted as if she herself were truly invulnerable. In the course of talking to her, I discussed the Hershey incident at length, and she volunteered to go there for me. (I hadn't the money or the manpower to leave a man there after I left.)

It took Mary Schneider only a few weeks in Hershey to establish a rapport with the factory workers and the Italian farm hands, partly by holding small meetings in the back room of an Italian grocery whose owner had taken a shine to her. We began to make plans to go ahead with a full-scale organizing drive.

One fine summer evening, Mary called me at home in Flourtown asking that I speak the following evening at an open-air meeting to be held in a field a few miles outside of Hershey that a farmer had agreed to rent to us. I agreed and was driven up the next afternoon by some of my young volunteers, Harold Ash, Sidney Schulman, and Robert Wolfe. (Wolfe's father was a successful corporation lawyer in Philadelphia as well as an outstanding Shakespearean scholar, and while I'm sure he regarded his son's decision to work for me as a piece of lunacy, he had given the young man two one-hundred-dollar bills to be used as bail in case the need arose.)

We held the meeting, I made my speech, and as the sun began to set, our audience began to drift away. Mary, our volunteers, and I, along with four or five others, remained standing around talking, and presently we noticed that a number of cars, each with three or four rough-looking characters in it, had driven up to the perimeter of the field and that the men were slowly drifting around us in a circle.

They began to jeer at us.

"Whadda you furriners doin' here?"

"Who gave you the right to be here?"

"We ain't gonna have your kind comin' in here to Hershey."

"You're gonna get outta here and never come back."

Then all of us saw that a couple of men had built a fire and were heating on it a big iron pot full of tar. We could smell it. Another had a fair-sized burlap bag, and he cut it open. It was full of feathers.

I can't explain the exact feelings I had. I found it hard to comprehend what was happening. I had read about tar-and-feathering. Now it was real. I hadn't the faintest idea of what to do, except that it would have been folly to stand there and do nothing. I started to walk toward the men, and Mary Schneider, imperturable as ever, fell in beside me. We headed for the man who seemed to be the leader of the group. I began an exhortation about mob violence, but Mary calmly began to explain that our meeting had been held under the guarantees of both the United States and Pennsylvania Constitutions, and that what these men were apparently intent upon seemed like the law of the jungle. Her words, gently spoken as always, stopped them. The leader looked at me.

"You're here, too," he said.

While the tar pot began to seethe, he turned away. I'm sure that the mob had started off with the full intention of tar-and-feathering us, but faced with an elderly imperturable widow and someone whose face they had seen in photographs in the newspapers, they began to realize that their idea wasn't quite as simple as it had seemed.

Finally, the leader returned and said, "Okay, all you goddamned people, get in your cars and get out of here and never come back."

I made what surely must be one of my most fatuous remarks ever. I said, "We have to go back into Hershey to pay our hotel bill."

Somehow, this seemed to relax everything. We got into our

two cars and drove back into Hershey—followed by all the cars of the mob. I went inside to pay the bill. While the hotel clerk was making it out, from a pay telephone in the lobby I called the governor to tell him what was happening.

He said, "Take your time paying the bill, and when you leave, take the main route to Philadelphia. Drive slowly. By the time you reach the Hershey city limits, I'll have a couple of state police cars there."

I did as I was told, and sure enough, at the city limits, there were the state police cars. We had been trailed by the mob cars, and the police stopped us all. I heard the state trooper go back to the driver of the first mob car and say, "Okay, fellows, it's all over. Turn the cars around and go home."

And they did. The state police escorted us all the way to Philadelphia, and finally, in the end, we organized the Hershey plant. The near tar-and-feathering had gotten the company officials extremely worried about what would have happened to the company's reputation if it really had been carried out.

On another occasion my reputation around Philadelphia paid off in avoiding violence. We were organzing a Ford assembly plant in Chester, and Harry Bennett's thugs were beating up our organizers every time they attempted to hand out leaflets at the plant gates. I found that if I announced to the newspapers that I was going to the plant to hand out the leaflets, and I was able to get a couple of reporters to go along with me, there would almost never be any violence.

In fact, I was absolutely startled one day to get a telephone call from the mayor's office telling me that I had been threatened with other violence—not by an employer but by the Teamsters Union. The police were prepared to provide me with a plainclothesman bodyguard, the mayor's office said, but the plainclothesman could not cross the city limits, and therefore would I please be prepared to stay inside the city limits until they felt that the threat had passed.

At first I was not disposed to take this threat seriously. Then, through union sources, I learned that the fledgling CIO had formed a local in a bakery in which the Teamsters already had a "sweetheart" contract. The employer had complained to the Teamsters, and the Teamsters had given the word to "get Edelman."

So for several weeks I lived in a hotel room in Philadelphia. The only time that I saw my family was in the North Philadelphia railroad waiting room where they came to visit me—and to bring me fresh clothes and laundry. It wasn't very romantic.

A long time afterward I ran into the head of the Philadelphia Teamsters in a hotel lobby in Washington, and he threw his arm around my shoulders.

"John," he said, beginning to cry, "you remember that time in Philadelphia? God, I honestly don't know what got into me. I always liked you so much!"

I hadn't understood it, either.

After we had the first score or so of new CIO locals on a functioning basis in Philadelphia, I was able to help establish a citywide CIO Council. I presided over it myself at first—one of the more rewarding duties of being the director of an organization—and also took part in launching the state CIO council.

But even as I was enjoying whatever success the fledgling CIO was beginning to achieve, my own storm signals were becoming ominous. I was getting into serious trouble with John L. Lewis.

First, I had a fullblown fight with Lewis about hotel workers in Atlantic City. What started it off was typical of what happens in any organization when the great man takes off on his own, then runs into a situation which he decides to put to rights without, of course, knowing the first thing about it. Lewis had spent a weekend at one of the fancy oceanfront hotels in Atlantic City, during the course of which he had been waited upon by a delegation of six waiters who fed him a long cock-and-bull story about how all the hotel workers were just waiting for the right leadership to rebuild the unions on the boardwalk.

That I knew a little about the hotel labor situation in Atlantic City was the main reason I avoided it. If the hotel business in Philadelphia was desperate, in Atlantic City it had been all put plowed under and sowed with salt. It was a disaster area. Moreover, the shell of the old union there was one hundred percent communist. Even if we had been able to revive the union, we would simply have been turning it over to the communists, not to the CIO. And the communists *hadn't* been able to rebuild it, despite help from their headquarters in New York.

I told Lewis all this at some length and got the sharp edge of his tongue in return. He all but told me in so many words that he'd had plently of experience with weak-spined AFL organizers who were afraid to tackle a situation that looked tough. That had been the trouble with the old AFL, and that was why—and so on.

So off I went to Atlantic City—in the dead of winter, when it looked like a deserted mining town—to spend an absolutely wasted month that could have been put to much better advantage in Philadelphia. I ran one miserable, ineffectual strike in one hotel, which I lost; I had a continual running fight with the police; I spent a third of my time raising bail money for the pickets; and I accomplished absolutely nothing.

I wrote Lewis a series of reports in which I tried to tell him, as politely as I could, that we'd all have been better off if he had stayed in Washington, handled the big issues, and stopped going to Atlantic City. Finally, even he agreed to abandon the organization drive, but the next time I saw him, he wouldn't talk to me. I got one of his famous scowls, and that was all.

That was the minor issue, however. There was a much more fundamental problem developing. The communists in some of my Philadelphia locals were taking over. My old word-of-mouth agreement with Pat Tuohy had gone out the window, as I had known it would the instant the communists saw a chance to take over.

Even though I had foreseen this, I began to get madder and madder. I had personally organized a number of these locals and had negotiated the first contracts. But the communists were now trading on my name and reputation, constantly saying, "Well, John Edelman told us. . . ." They also were introducing all sorts of communist propaganda and "educational" material into the meetings and into the shop papers of these locals.

What made this sort of thing so important, I thought, was that I could foresee the communists soon moving in on whole international unions of the CIO, taking them over—as they actually did with the Electrical Workers and might have with the Auto Workers had it not been for Walter Reuther, his brothers Victor and Roy, plus a handful of other top officials—possibly taking over even the whole CIO itself.

I talked to Lewis and said that, as far as the Philadelphia locals were concerned, I would go back in and clean them out. I would attend the local meetings and tell the workers what was going on, that my name was being taken in vain, that I was strongly anticommunist, that I did not want to see this labor movement subverted by the communists. I told Lewis that I thought my name carried enough weight that the workers would listen to me. Also, I would have fired out of hand about a dozen business agents. We at CIO headquarters could not interfere with local officials of the local unions, for they had been duly elected by the members (except to warn the members against those who were so transparently communists, as I proposed to do). But business agents, who supervised the day-to-day running of the contracts, were officers of the CIO, employed by us and paid by us. They could be—and would be, if I had my way—fired immediately.

What drove me wild with frustration about Lewis was that I simply could not get him to discuss this problem seriously. He knew it could mean trouble as well as I did. I had as much admiration for him then as I do now. Who else but Lewis would have dared to spend millions of dollars out of the treasury of the UMW, in the midst of the worst depression in the history of the industrialized world, on a sheer gamble that the mass-production workers could be organized?

With his physical size—over six feet, 220 pounds—huge fists, long arms, his flamboyant eyebrows (red, when I first knew him), the perpetual scowl, the outthrust jaw, the ever-present cigar, the tilted-down hat; with his talent as a public performer and all his classical and Biblical allusions (who but Lewis, after Franklin Roosevelt publicly washed his hands of the steel dispute by saying of labor and management, "A plague o' both their houses," would have answered, "It ill befits one who has supped at the table of labor to ignore their cry for bread"?), with his daring and skill as a negotiator with the mine owners—as piratical a bunch as ever inhabited the face of the earth—Lewis was almost the equal of FDR, in the thirties, as a public figure.

Lewis knew that the basic drive of the communists was to gain power. He knew that he was as smart as the communists, if not smarter, and just as tough, if not tougher.

When I confronted him with all the worries I had about them, and what they might do to the CIO, all I could get was a shrug and the answer, "I know how to handle them. I've handled them before."

I knew what that meant. For years, the communists had tried to get power in the coal mines of the country, particularly in western Pennsylvania. What Lewis did was simply to have them beaten up, then blackballed so that they couldn't get jobs. A couple of times, indeed, I had even gone to local UMW headquarters, simply on the basis of human charity, and asked them to put back to work men they had blackballed.

I argued as strongly as I could with Lewis that this way of "handling" the communists might be the way to do it in the UMW with three hundred thousand members, mostly rough, tough workers sophisticated in labor matters, but what was he going to do when the CIO got to be a union of three, four, or five million workers scattered all over the country, many of them insurance agents, newspaper reporters, welfare workers, and store clerks?

To that—as I regarded it—basic question, I never could get an answer from Lewis. I think that he simply didn't want to face it.

Lewis's attitude discouraged me almost as much as the problems I was having with the communists in Philadelphia, and that attitude was probably the deciding factor in my decision to leave the Philadelphia CIO.

But there were two other factors. The first was that Kate had had an excellent job offer from the USHA in Washington, and she was anxious to take it. Because of her work in planning for community facilities at the Carl Mackley Houses in Philadelphia, she had been asked to become an adviser on community planning for the USHA. The job would require her living in Washington, and—odd as this must sound in view of all the traveling that I had been doing for years and years—we could not face up to living in two cities a hundred and fifty miles apart indefinitely. The children, too—what would it do to them?

Also, I was becoming physically exhausted. It is possible to operate on nervous energy for just so long. It could keep me going for sixteen to twenty hours a day when I was organizing, negotiating, moving, but now that a certain amount of order was coming into our work, I suddenly realized that I had been driving myself for far too long.

There were two ways to solve the problem. One was to have a really good, out-and-out fight with Lewis, which I obviously would have lost. The other was to just plain quit. So, late in the spring of 1939, after almost three solid years with the CIO in Philadelphia, I quit.

Chapter Ten

WHEN I QUIT the Pennsylvania CIO, I went to work as a lobbyist for the USHA in Washington. It was a logical move. I had been lobbying, as part of my labor jobs, for over fifteen years. I had been a member of an advisory committee to the FHA in the early days of the New Deal. And USHA had been in political trouble almost from the moment that the enabling legislation had first been signed because of the bitter opposition of the organized real estate interests and their lobbies. Leon Keyserling, my old friend who had been Sen. Robert Wagner's chief assistant, had become assistant administrator of USHA and thought that I might help if I came in with the title of assistant director of public relations. But what I was really supposed to do was to help USHA up on Capitol Hill.

There are all sorts of regulations against government emloyees lobbying, but I don't know of a single government agency that doesn't lobby in one way or another. In fact, the heads of some government agencies have been named to their jobs simply *because* of the weight they carry on the Hill.

I had a short and not particularly sweet career at USHA.

My problem was with the administrator, Nathan Straus. Straus had many good qualities. He was a member of the rich New York family that owned R. H. Macy & Co., he engaged in philanthropic activities, was a liberal and a very early supporter of Franklin Roosevelt, which is how he became Housing Administrator. Opposed to his good qualities, however, was the fact that he was a very self-important man. I got off on the wrong foot right from the start.

Problem one was that, while Straus regarded himself an expert in public housing, Keyserling hadn't bothered to tell him that I was being hired. Since my reputation in the field was more impressive than Straus's, the situation had already become a bit sticky before I even showed up in the office.

Strangely, Straus also resented the fact that the Carl Mackley Houses in Philadelphia were regarded as an outstanding architectural and planning project, while a much larger project that he had sponsored in New York was not.

Another problem arose from a casual comment by a congressman, a member of the House Banking and Currency Committee. When Straus and I walked in together at the start of a committee hearing on USHA, this friend remarked, "You needn't have bothered to come all the way up here for this, Nathan. John can tell us everything we need to know."

It didn't take much brain power on my part to recognize that no boss, much less Straus, was going to have an employee like me around very long, and I wasn't.

I don't want to cite my own problems with the USHA as the perfect example of how the bureaucracy of the federal government fails to use the brains it has available to it, although I feel deeply about it, so I'll cite the cases of three other former government employees.

One of the early casualties among government agencies, when the first glamour of the New Deal had worn off, was the liquidation of the National Resources Planning Board, (NRPB), which included a staff of brilliant economists. Their reports on the state of natural resources had annoyed a number of prominent industrialists, and it was largely as a result of this opposition that the board was dissolved. Several of the economists joined forces to form a private economic-counseling service in Washington, which soon became a thriving business. One of them, Gardiner Means, said to me, "John, it just goes to show you the brain power of the average top industry executive. When I was working for the government, they got all this information free. Now I charge them a fine fat fee for the same information, and they love it. So do I."

Then Morris Llewellyn Cooke was appointed (by Franklin Roosevelt) chairman of a commission to study the feasibility of establishing a Mississippi Valley Authority, similar to the TVA. The project was opposed by the Army Corps of Engineers. At one of the early meetings, Cooke told the other members of the commission, "I like to present facts graphically, therefore I have prepared a map to illustrate the problems we face, showing the water flow from each of its tributaries into the Mississippi." After a period of study, one of the members asked, "But why are all the Corps of Engineers studies aimed at the west bank, when this map shows that the big flow of water comes in from the rivers on the east bank?"

Louis Bean, a brilliant statistical analyst for the Department of Agriculture projecting crop production for years (he had gone to work for the department during the administration of Calvin Coolidge), correctly predicted the election of Harry S Truman in 1948 (using the same methods he had in the department). When Eisenhower was elected in 1952, Bean was fired, obviously because of the Truman report. Like the NRPB economists, Bean started his own business in Washington and soon was charging private industry the "fine fat fees" for work it had earlier gotten free.

Leon Keyserling took much of the blame for my problem at USHA upon himself, and refused to allow me to be fired. By this time, the Office of Price Administration (OPA) had been established, and Leon Henderson, whom I had known since he had worked for Governor Pinchot in Pennsylvania, had been put in charge. (With the inevitable entry of the United States into World War II now obvious, the OPA had been established in April of 1941.) Henderson, who had been a professor of economics at the University of Pennsylvania, had originally come to Washington to work in the NRA for Gen. Hugh Johnson. The story I heard was that Leon had been so pertinacious in his defense of consumer interests in the NRA that Johnson had shouted at him, "Goddamn it, I'll set up a special goddamn department just for you to run for your goddamn consumers!" And that was how the OPA was born.

I had talked to Henderson a number of times about my belief that labor had to be represented on his new agency and—I like to think that it was partly through my persuasion—the OPA became the first government agency to have a labor office.

The office was to be headed by a "neutral" representative—he turned out to be Robert R. R. Brooks ("Triple R Brooks"), a brilliant and elegant professor of economics at Williams College—and was to include a CIO representative, an AFL representative. and a representative of the Brotherhood of Railway Unions.

I was nominated as the CIO representative, but for a few weeks it was touch and go. The reason for this was one of those experiences that requires the most mind-rending decision I know—between right and right.

I had gone to a conference at the University of Pittsburgh to speak on the role of labor as protector of the consumer's rights. There, I had been put on the spot by an old UMW friend, Patrick J. Fagan, then a Pittsburgh city councilman and an official of the CIO.

Fagan demanded, at the conference, that I state where I stood on the question of allowing an increase in the wages of steel workers, which the union was then pressing. This would have meant "bending" the wage stabilization formula. Fagan knew as well as I that I could hardly turn my back on the government's policy of controlling inflation by regulating both wages and profits. Yet how would I have looked, as a labor man, saying at a public meeting, in front of some fairly hostile reporters, that I thought the union demands were unjustified?

I did the only thing I could at the time and the place. I told Fagan that in view of the extraordinary increases in steel productivity at that time I saw no justification for automatic rises in steel prices that the steel companies would demand to justify the wage increases.

This answer satisfied most of the people at the conference, but it did not satisfy my old friend Fagan, who immediately telephoned Philip Murray to report that I had hedged in my support of the steelworkers' position.

Fortunately, Harold Ruttenberg, then research director for the Steel Workers and a protégé of mine from years back, tipped me off to what was going on, and I immediately went to see Murray. This, in turn, embarrassed Murray. Whom should he support between two old labor friends? He turned the matter back to Ruttenberg for advice, and luckily for me there was a stenographic record of the conference, which I turned over to Harold. A few days later Murray recommended me to Henderson as CIO representative at the OPA labor office.

My co-members in the office were John Burk for the AFL, and, for the Railway Brotherhood, the late Glenn Atkinson, research director for the Railway Clerks, an ex-socialist and a graduate of Brookwood Labor College. In addition, Henderson had two personal labor advisers, my old friend Boris Shiskin of the AFL, and Raymond Walsh of the CIO. Their advice, however, was generally on the top level of the relationship of the OPA to the trade-union movement, whereas our office was a day-to-day operation concerned with presenting the labor point of view on almost every problem over which the OPA had jurisdiction, from price controls to rationing. Fortunately, Burk, Atkinson, Shiskin, Walsh, and I got along very well personally and saw eye to eye on most issues. Also, we were in an agency that was receptive to listening to the labor point of view, from Henderson on down.

One constructive accomplishment of which I am proud was getting a woman named Edith Christenson to work for us. I had known her since the Hosiery days in Pennsylvania, when she had undertaken some tough organizing jobs for us, and she had gone to work for the Women's Trade Union League

(WTUL). I had been racking my brain to try to find some way to explain rationing and price controls to the families of workers. After the WTUL was discontinued, Miss Christenson had gone to work for the Wage and Hour Administration, but I was able to get her to come to the OPA. There, she did herculean labor in getting wives and families of workers to understand the necessity for OPA.

That, in fact, was one of the major jobs that we in the labor office of OPA faced, not only with the workers and their families but also with local trade-union officers. All these people—and no one knew better than I—felt that "price-fixing" simply meant that the government had gone into cahoots with management to try to keep wages down.

I think that one of the major strokes of genius in getting labor to understand what the OPA was doing was the OPA's top leadership decision to see to it that a labor man was appointed to every one of its boards throughout the country. It was easy, and understandable, for labor to complain about "price-fixing" and to demand inflationary wage increases when it was outside the OPA. When labor representatives were brought into the decision-making process, however, it became another matter.

But making sure that labor men were appointed to the OPA boards was of itself almost a full-time job for our office; we were continually getting complaints from around the country that local boards were refusing to comply with the ruling, or simply ignoring it.

Two of the situations that I was assigned to deal with remain in my mind. The first was in Williamsport, in northern Pennsylvania, a notoriously bitter antilabor town since the 1920s when the local businessmen had organized vigilante groups to drive union organizers out of town. I speak from personal experience; I was one of those driven out. But now here I came to Williamsport, an official of the OPA from Washington, guest of honor at a luncheon given by the Chamber of Commerce.

I would be considerably more than human if I did not admit that I watched the expressions of the luncheon guests as

I was introduced, with full attention given to my background as a former organizer for the Hosiery Workers in Williamsport. I must add, however, that in this time of war the former rancor seemed to have disappeared. I behaved in a most seemly manner and spoke in most tactful and patriotic terms about the necessity for having all segments of society represented on the rationing boards—including labor. The audience applauded heartily and agreed that labor would be represented.

The second situation occurred just outside Roanoke, Virginia. There, Charles Webber, a Methodist clergyman, president of the state CIO council and an organizer for the ACW, was running into the same old troubles: A loosely knit organization of employers, business leaders, the local Ku Klux Klan, and the police was preventing him from holding meetings.

It was strictly against OPA policy for one of its paid employees to become involved in anything like this, but when Charles called me at home and told me what was happening, I checked with Henderson to make sure that I would not be embarrassing him, then went down to a meeting of local leaders that Webber had arranged to speak to on how it was a matter of federal government policy to encourage labor to take a full role in helping win the war, and so on. My God, how times had changed!

Despite the irregularity of my intervening in such a situation, the desired end was achieved. Webber was allowed to go ahead with his meetings, which eventually resulted in the establishment of a collective-bargaining system in the plants, and a labor man was quietly added to the membership of the local rationing board.

Another major problem with which I was involved in the OPA was one of great, though at that time practically unnoticed, significance. One of the banes of the labor movement for decades had been company housing—the practice of mills and factories of throwing up ramshackle and indescribably disreputable rows of the cheapest sort of houses imaginable, with neither facilities nor amenities of any sort, and charging exorbitant rents. Private housing contractors never even entered the picture because the scale of wages paid mill workers meant that those workers could not possibly afford to build even the cheapest houses. Most of the mill houses were three- or four-room shacks with wood-burning stoves; no insulation of any kind in the walls or under the floors; toilets were privies in the back yard; water was carried from a tap in a pipe that ran down the center of the settlement; there were no electric lights, no sidewalks, or paved roads. Rent in the 1920s and 1930s was twenty-four cents per room per week, deducted from wages in advance.

In the early days of World War II in this country, with so many workers getting "rich" compared to their former standards, some companies got the brilliant idea of selling these ramshackle houses to their occupants. The plan came to my attention through a telephone call one night from a man named Edward Ryan, business agent for the Textile Workers at a group of mills owned by the Marshall Field department store company in three small, adjoining communities in northwestern North Carolina named Draper, Leaksville, and Spray. They have since incorporated into one town, which, by referendum, named itself Eden. Ryan had once been a student of mine in workers' education classes and had gotten my telephone number simply by calling information.

Ryan had a problem, he told me, and union headquarters in New York was too busy to do anything about it. The Marshall Field company, Ryan felt, was being taken in by a shyster real estate operator who had sold them on the advantages of getting rid of their houses and who now was pressuring the mill workers to buy them at anywhere from three to four times their value. The pressure consisted of telling the workers that if they didn't buy, they'd have to move out. This, in a mill town in wartime in which there wasn't any other housing at all. When I had been research director at Hosiery, we had found that the average mill owner had made an average investment of less than two thousand dollars per house and that at the start of World War II, the average house had been paid for at least twice over, including interest at twelve percent. These houses were now being offered to the workers at from six to eight thousand dollars each.

Rent control was a legitimate concern of the OPA, but this operation was a little far removed from rent control. Nonetheless, when Ryan told me about his problem, I decided to look into the situation in North Carolina for myself.

I did take the precaution of explaining the whole situation to Tom Tippett, a Brookwood Labor College alumnus, author of *When Southern Labor Stirs,* and—most important—the second-in-command of the rent-control division of OPA. I was also aware that Tom was a friend of Marshall Field's.

In North Carolina I spent two days walking around the villages and talking to the people. What horrified me was not so much the houses—they were bad enough, but by no means as bad as many with which I was more familiar—but the method of payment that the real estate operator had been able to talk the Marshall Field company into. This was one dollar a day per room, to be deducted from workers' wages in advance.

On my second day in the neighborhood I got in touch with the manager of the plants, Luther Hodges, later governor of the state and secretary of commerce for President John F. Kennedy. I explained to Hodges that labor fully appreciated Marshall Field's desire to get out of the landlord business but that the company, as well as the workers, was being taken for a ride. I suggested that Hodges go ahead with the company plan but that he make the selling agent of the houses the real estate brokers' association in nearby Greensboro and establish the normal procedure for buying houses: granting mortgages and having the buyer make his payments directly to the mortgagor (or his agent) rather than having it deducted from the buyer's wages.

Hodges agreed to put my plan into operation, and it worked out extremely well. The Marshall Field company was pleased; the local real estate and mortgage people were pleased; and when I returned there a number of years later, it was obvious that the workers had been pleased. Instead of a collection of worthless old ramshackle houses, I found a handsome-looking community of well-kept, neatly painted homes, each with a lawn, most of them with garages. The old-time privies were gone, the streets were paved, sidewalks had been built, electric lights illuminated the whole town. Walking the streets, I felt almost is if I had done the whole thing myself.

The town of Eden is but one instance—I have cited it because of my own role there—of the great revolution that took place in the "company town" pattern of housing brought about by World War II. I am well aware that "company towns," and far too many of them, exist even today in the United States. But they are no longer the usual pattern. There are many reasons for the changes: the unions, the concept of public housing, the war, crusading journalists. But the most important change, I believe, is in the changing pattern of American life and in the American way of thinking. In the twenties and thirties, the "company town" was an accepted way of life. It did, in fact, have a great many defenders who made cases to prove that these towns demonstrated the social awareness of business management. (Actually, there were some instances in which this was true.) But today, in the national consciousness, the "company town" is not accepted.

At this time during my career in the OPA, Emil Rieve telephoned me in Washington from his office in New York.

Rieve had been elected president of the Textile Workers Union of America (TWUA) and had established a Washington office to represent it on legislative matters. The Washington office was headed by one of the most vigorous and dashing union men I ever knew—Robert Oliver, who had begun his labor career with the Oil Workers but had switched to Textiles because he thought that there were not enough battles to be fought for the Oil Workers. In 1943, with a war on, Oliver—despite a job, a wife, his children, and his age (he was forty)—wanted even tougher battles to fight. So he had resigned from Textiles to enlist in the army as a private.

That left his Washington job open, and Rieve called me up to New York to pressure me into taking it. He told me that I simply had to get out of government and return to the labor movement. As an added inducement, he offered me a reduction in salary.

Naturally, I accepted.

Chapter Eleven

I WAS GETTING into a far more complicated field than I realized when I said yes to Rieve.

One factor was that not all of the former AFL Textile Workers officers had gone with Rieve into his CIO TWUA when the AFL-CIO split had developed. There had been an ugly power struggle between Rieve and the old AFL Textile president, Francis Gorman. Rieve had won, but Gorman and his followers—and his locals—had remained in the AFL. To this day, there is still a textile union in the AFL, called the United Textile Workers. It is approximately one-fourth the size of the TWUA, and whatever the merits or demerits of the differences that led to the split, I feel that it weakened the strength of organized labor as a whole.

As "legislative agent," which I called myself, for the Textile Workers, I automatically became a member of the newly established Legislative Committee of the CIO, headed by Nathan Cowan, a veteran UMW official whom I had known since my early days in Pennsylvania. Philip Murray had made Cowan chairman of the Legislative Committee, and he was therefore my day-to-day boss. Rieve, of course, was paying my salary, and I was finally responsible to him.

I find it somewhat ironic that the building in which the Legislative Committee met was at 718 Jackson Place, the one-block-long street facing on LaFayette Square, the tiny park that is directly across Pennsylvania Avenue from the White House. The building had long been the headquarters of the Republican National Committee, but it had been sold to the CIO during the Depression. For years, Joseph W. Martin, speaker of the House, used to grumble to me about the "fast deal" that Phil Murray and the whole labor "crowd" had pulled in buying the building at a time when the country, and especially the Republican party, was on its uppers.

The two immediate tasks that I faced as I began my initial full-time venture into lobbying were drearily prosaic. First, I was faced with setting up an office for myself; second, I had to get to know the new Textile Workers officials, those who had advanced in the union in the seven years that I had been away. During those years the union had vastly changed. It had grown enormously, especially in New England, in New York State, and in the Midwest. It had even carved out a precarious toehold in the South. Except for the top echelon of the union officials, I had not even met most of the local officers who had brought about this growth.

In the middle of a world war, with tooth-and-nail fighting for office space in downtown Washington, finding an office was no easy task. There was absolutely no room in the CIO Jackson Place headquarters, but fortunately I was able to sublet some space from a couple of old friends, Paul and Claire Sifton. Paul at one time had been city editor of the old *New York World* and had later been the top publicist for Norman Thomas's campaign for the presidency in 1932. In 1943, Paul and his wife were *the* Washington office of the Union for Democratic Action (UDA), the forerunner of the current Americans for Democratic Action.

But only a few months after I had moved into the Sifton offices, the UDA gave up the ghost, and my sublet had no meaning. I had to look for new quarters. Once again, the

Amalgamated Clothing Workers came to the aid of Textiles. The Amalgamated had a set of offices in the Warner Building, above the Warner (motion picture) Theater at E and 13th Streets, which they had originally rented to provide office space for their lawyers to handle wage-and-hour enforcement problems (the first, and, so far as I know, only union to do this). The Amalgamated agreed to sublet a couple of their offices to Textiles, and I was able to move in.

With my office space finally set, my next three major needs were a secretary, some furniture, and a telephone.

Secretaries for an office like mine were almost as hard to find as the office itself. All of the young women in Washington then wanted to work in the War Department or some other glamorous government agency in which there were plenty of young men. They didn't want to work in a one-man labor office for a boss who was fifty years old with a wife and three grown children. (Our oldest, Alison, had been graduated from Sarah Lawrence College in 1942 and was working as an aluminum welder for the Douglas Aircraft Company in Los Angeles. A Class A welder, she proudly wrote home, which meant that she was making $1.25 an hour instead of 65 cents on the assembly line. Arnold had completed his freshman year at Harvard and had left to join the Army Air Corps where he had become a bomber pilot. Our youngest, Anne, was an undergraduate at Sarah Lawrence.)

My sister Sonia had sent her three children over to us from London shortly after the war had begun. The oldest, John, a pacifist like myself by instinct and training, later volunteered for the Royal Air Force and became a bomber pilot; he was killed in a raid over Germany. Sonia's daughter Barbara was eighteen and a student at George Washington University. The youngest child, Richard, now editor of the *Tribune* in London, the weekly newspaper that is the voice of the left wing of the Labour Party, was in high school. It was my niece Barbara whom I recruited as part-time secretary. Her first job was to scrounge through secondhand office-furnishing stores in Washington looking for filing cabinets, desks, and chairs.

It was also a major piece of lobbying in those days to obtain a telephone, but eventually we did, and I was ready to go to work.

Two essential needs coincided at this point, and I was gradually able to satisfy both of them. The first, as I mentioned, was to get to know the district and local officers of the union better; the second was to have an accurate count of membership, local by local and district by district. While there are always a certain number of congressmen with whom you can argue legislation solely on its merits, a certain number are so circumscribed in their own thinking, emotions, or prejudices that it is worthless to spend your time talking to them at all; however, the great majority will listen to you if you can show them where the votes are. It is a great advantage if a lobbyist can start off a discussion about a piece of legislation by saying, "You know, Jack (or whatever his name is), the union is very much interested in trying to pass this bill, and there are X thousand textile workers in your district."

It's never quite that crass, of course. Any congressman worth his salt knows, or should know, his own district better than any lobbyist. (Though a surprising number of congressmen can be surprisingly dense.) But in lobbying for a vote on any specific issue, a lobbyist simply has to know what strength he has behind him, and the strength that a congressman understands best is the number of votes that can be mustered for or against him the next time he runs. In addition, I found as the years went by, bills were getting so complicated and so technical that if I could get our research staff to break them down and explain their possible consequences, I was actually performing a service for the congressman. No congressman can afford a staff big enough and sophisticated enough to explain the provisions of every bill to him.

So, in order for me to have the vote picture at my fingertips, it was necessary for me to get a breakdown of Textile Union membership by locals, districts, and states.

Here I ran up against what I might call cultural lag. When I started to try to assemble my membership breakdowns, I soon found that I was up against the ancient trade-union practice of never letting anyone see the membership lists.

There once had been two sound reasons for that. The first was that if management learned the names of employees who had joined a union, they would summarily be fired. The second was that, in the old days, local unions consistently reported their membership as greater than it actually was to give them greater leverage in bargaining situations.

All of this had made sense twenty or thirty years earlier, but at this moment in time I was concerned with a problem in which this kind of thinking was of no use whatsoever. There were other stumbling blocks, such as the endemic problem of plain human laziness, but slowly, over a period of months, I was able to get together a workable list of names and addresses of Textile Union members, broken down into congressional voting districts.

By this time, my job was beginning to assume a pattern of two distinct parts, which I came to refer to as my "regular job" and my "weekend job."

My regular job was working as a lobbyist in Washington. My weekend job, while perhaps not as substantively important, was necessary. It consisted of visiting as many local unions around the country as I could. Even during wartime, with all the difficulties of transportation—gas rationing, getting space on trains, and so on—I was traveling twenty-five thousand miles a year.

But it was necessary. As I have said, I felt it my duty to visit the various locals, to let the local officers and membership see what I looked like and to hear what I had to say. In the final analysis, they were paying my salary. It's too easy for a lobbyist, or a newspaperman, to fall into the pleasant and rewarding life of being a "Washington representative" and begin to forget the workaday reality of the lives of the people he's supposed to be representing.

Second, it provided me with an invaluable opportunity for discussion. While I could explain what we were doing in Washington, the local people could tell me what their problems were. In a small way, I was doing some missionary work. I was firmly convinced that unless local people were aware of, and had some insight into, the legislative process, I would be wasting my time in Washington. And when I returned to Washington, what I had heard in the field was equally important in talking to people on the Hill.

Lobbying is a continuous process. You can't wait until some piece of legislation in which you have an interest is about to be passed, then decide that you'll try to affect the vote in Congress by getting a thousand signatures on a petition. Most congressmen regard most mass petitions as so many rolls of waste paper, and rightly so. Without too much trouble, an experienced set of canvassers can get you ten thousand signatures on *any* petition in a relatively short span of time.

The only way to impress a congressman with a petition is first to explain that *all* the signers are registered voters in his district. Then you tell him when and where the signatures were obtained. Then, if possible, you have every signer list his occupation. If, for example, the petition concerns legislation affecting the textile industry, and you get a thousand filling-station owners to sign it, the congressman is going to thank you. Nothing more. But if you get a thousand knitting machine operators to sign it, he's going to listen.

And you cannot confine yourself to election time, making sure your man gets in. Lobbying is, to repeat, a continuous process. A good lobbyist should know almost as much about how the legislative process works as an experienced congressman; *really* know how it works. Congressional bills do not just somehow magically appear out of the everywhere into the here. The legislative process is long, complicated, and tedious. But for all its defects it is, so far as I know, the only workable system of getting truly democratic legislation.

To have a hope of passage, a bill must either answer an obvious and pressing social need, or it must have considerable political muscle behind it. Preferably both. All of the social legislation that has been passed by Congress since the beginning of the thirties falls, I believe, into the first classification. All of the oil-depletion-allowance bills, all of the so-called "pork barrel" bills, and most of the maritime and transportation (especially highway transportation) legislation fall into the second.

Part of the reason that I originally gave myself the title of legislative representative was that, while most of my interest would be directed toward legislative matters, I knew also that I would spend a good deal of time representing the union before government agencies.

Rieve, for example, was a member of the War Labor Board, but he (with me as a kind of secretary general) would normally participate only in the major policy-making meetings of the board. The day-to-day work with the agency in dealing with all the terribly complicated labor-management problems of that period was left entirely to me.

There was a host of other government agencies I had to deal with. The NLRB was the next most important—toward the end of my career it became the most important—but there were many others: the Labor Department, Housing, so many I could not list them.

I could guess that lobbying, like most other work, is at a minimum devoted half to doing things that seem nonproductive—writing letters, making phone calls, attending meetings, working on projects that frustrate you because, while doing them, you always have the feeling that you should be doing something more important.

I remember one case in which I was involved that illustrates my point.

The Textile Union had organized a small plant in Ohio that processed "wiping cloths." Many industries use "wiping cloths," which are exactly what the name says, pieces of cloth that are used to wipe things up. If you're running a fair-sized machine shop, you may need a ton of them a week, and you want them all roughly the same size—to your specifications—and above all you want them clean.

Our small Ohio plant bought all sorts of remnants of cloth, cut them to the required sizes, washed them, baled them, and sold them. One of the plant's major customers was the quartermaster corps of the army, and in one shipment to an army installation the remnants of some American flags were found.

There are specific rules for the disposal of worn-out American flags—"burning in a private place" is the generally recommended one—but cutting them up for wiping cloths is definitely not on the list. The army took a very dim view of the situation. It instituted a suit against the Ohio plant that would have forever prevented it from doing business with the government, which would have effectively put the plant out of business and about fifty of our members out of work. It turned out that the plant had processed the cloths in all innocence. It had bought the worthless remnants of material from a company that made flags.

This tiny case kicked around the Pentagon for almost two years. I must have made at least fifty phone calls before I was able to get someone in the Pentagon to *listen* to me who *also* had the authority to do something. But if I hadn't finally been able to get the action, of course, we would have lost the fifty members, and there would have been fifty workers firmly convinced that the union was no place to take their problems.

Just as the early Wagner Act had been of great help to the labor movement in its old organizing drives, so the new government agencies—and the whole increasing involvement of the labor movement with the government process as typified by Philip Murray's establishment of the Legislative Committee of the CIO—also helped the unions in protecting the rights of its own members. In the old days, to make my point as clearly as I can, if an employee felt that his employer was shortchanging him, he could complain to his shop steward, and the union would take the problem up with the employer. If the employer told the union to go to hell, there weren't too many other places to go, except on strike. But now the union had the power of the federal government behind it. It came down to the simple fact that a worker in a non-union plant could get a wage increase by the simple expedient of having a union come in.

When I first went to work for Textiles in Washington in 1943, the federally supported wage standards were still far too low.

The Fair Labor Standards Act, which set the minimum wage, had been passed during FDR's second term and signed on June 25, 1938. It had been many years on the way, and there is no point in describing its journey here. Today, its early achievements sound pitiful: forty cents an hour, to be reached in three stages, beginning in 1938 at twenty-five cents an hour.

A perpetually recurring problem in Textiles was to determine which shops and factories were covered by the Act. Our friend Edith Christenson, who worked in the New York office, told us a tale that illustrates the difficulty of reaching a fair decision. One morning her supervisor, James Kelly, asked her to handle a complaint that had come by letter from a woman who was employed as a seamstress in a Madison Avenue shop that made fine undergarments for women. The complaint was that although the work was highly skilled, the women were being paid less than the minimum wage. The woman did not sign her name, fearing that she would lose her job if the management learned she had complained. She asked further that no action be taken that would result in the shop's being closed, since all of the employees desperately needed their jobs. The letter had been addressed to Mrs. Roosevelt, a patron of the shop, and she had forwarded it to the New York Wage and Hour office for action. Edith pondered: Did the new law apply here? Just then the chief inspector of the office, Ray Jenkins, passed by.

"What are you puzzling over, Edie?" he asked. She showed him the letter. After a few seconds he handed it back.

"Hell!" he said. "Any shop that sells anything that Eleanor Roosevelt wears is engaged in interstate commerce!"

The story had a happy ending. Mr. Jenkins was able to convince the manager of the shop to adopt minimum wage levels without getting into official channels.

I recall a conversation I had on the Hill with John F. Kennedy, then a member of the House, during a drive we were conducting to extend minimum-wage coverage. After listening to my argument, Jack said almost pleadingly, "Oh, John, don't press me to do this. There are so few things I can do for the businessmen in Massachusetts, and this would hurt them."

"Okay, Jack," I said. "But I think you're going to be around here for a long time. And if you can live with yourself after you run out on this, I promise you I won't bother you again for a long, long time."

In the end, Jack went to bat for the bill, and though it failed to pass, I never again—even after he became president—had any trouble with John F. Kennedy about supporting minimum wage.

There were many other changes taking place in the economic patterns of the nation in those days, and I think that we in labor were too slow to recognize their implications. It was not simply the ever-increasing role of the government in the economic sector of the country—slowly becoming as important as either industry or labor. It was also that the war itself was radically altering the structure of the economy and of the whole industrial process. The impact on the aircraft and automobile industries is so obvious that comment would be superfluous, but it was equally true, in proportion, in the textile industry.

The Textile Workers were all too familiar with the upheavals that the introduction of synthetic materials had caused in the spinning industry. But the war had introduced a whole new element: The insatiable demand for textiles encouraged not only a speedup in the modernization of the machinery in existing mills but also proliferation of whole new plants, most of them in the South. In the South, it was the accepted economic practice to pay less than the going national rate for wages of any kind. For decades, the South had been a millstone around the neck of economic progress in the nation, and it is basically responsible for textile wages even today averaging seventy cents an hour lower than the average in other major industries.

Part of the blame for this must be put on the Wage-Hour Administration. The Administration had never been competent to enforce federal regulations in the textile industry, nor had it the will to try. The refusal of the big employers to pay any heed to the federal wage minimums, plus the ineffectiveness of the Administration in enforcing them, made almost all of the Textile attempts to organize the South totally ineffectual.

Within the framework of the changing pattern of the economic fabric of the nation, there were three constructive things that I was able to accomplish in those days. One was to enlarge the concept of coalition lobbying. There were a number of organizations lobbying in those days, generally to the same ends. I think that I helped to bring a number of them, and their representatives, together into a cohesive whole. There was the Amalgamated Clothing Workers (Esther Peterson); the ILGWU (Evelyn Dubrow); the District of Columbia Home Rule Committee (Kate Alfriend); the AFL (Andrew Biemiller, director of its legislative department); the National Consumers League (Mary Keyserling), and a host of others: Mary Alice Baldinger of the American Civil Liberties Union; Wallace Campbell of the Foundation for Cooperative Housing; the League of Women Voters; Olya Margolin of the Jewish Community Center; and Lee Johnson and Nat Keith of the National Housing Conference.

To coordinate the efforts of these various groups, I helped set up regular meetings to discuss our mutual objectives and to discuss our various strategies. We formed committees to give focus to our work—there would have been little point, for example, to have the Civil Liberties Union working at full strength on housing—and worked out which members of the Congress each one of us should concentrate on. This was how I happened to become the chairman of the Committee on Minimum Wages.

The second accomplishment was the establishment of the Textile Workers' annual legislative institute. The first of these institutes was set up in 1949 through the combined efforts of the TWUA education department, its political-action committee, and its legislative office. Its purpose was to inform rank-and-file workers more fully about their responsibilities as citizens and members of the union. Local unions were asked to choose one or two delegates to send to Washington to spend several days learning firsthand how the government works.

The Washington office organized the program in the Capitol —briefing sessions by top Textile officials; talks by other labor leaders, key officials of government agencies, and members of Congress; visits to committee hearings on legislation of special interest to them; visits to their own congressmen to discuss the legislation—and having their pictures taken with the congressman.

The third thing that I did was to adopt what came to be called the "victim witness" technique.

The issue at the time was the minimum wage. The big unions, although they paid lip service to it, weren't anywhere nearly as interested in minimum wage as were the people in textiles, clothing, and shoes. Big-union members were already getting well above the minimum wage.

And in lobbying, if one of the big unions wanted to make a splash with congressional testimony, it could always call in a Walter Reuther or a Philip Murray, whose words would be listened to with respect and whose testimony (along with the name of the committee chairman, which was important) would appear in all the papers the next day. I had no such resources.

When you were setting up testimony for one of my kind of hearings, you had to keep in mind the opposition's plan of action. I knew perfectly well that the textile industry was going to produce an endless series of textile-corporation officials and an equally endless series of tame economists, all of whom would testify at endless length and with innumerable charts and infinite statistics proving that to increase the minimum wage by so much as a nickel would plunge the entire industry, and possibly the entire nation, into bankruptcy. Again, I had no such resources.

Then, out of my remembrance of how carefully the average congressional committee tends to treat the nonprofessional witness, especially if there are newspapermen present, I began to build the concept of the "victim witness."

I could, I know, have gotten some college professors of economics to testify for us—there is nothing the average college professor likes so much as appearing as an expert witness before a congressional committee—but I knew from bitter experience that that would turn into nothing but a dreary exchange of statistics with the chairman saying something like, "Well, Professor, if your figures lead you to believe this, why do Dr. Blank's figures lead him to believe that?"

On the other hand, I knew that no chairman would be able to challenge the case of an average worker who could simply say, "Well, Mr. Chairman, I don't know nothing about figures, all I know is that I just plain can't bring up a family on fifty cents an hour."

Picking the witnesses I wanted to present was a great deal more difficult than I had foreseen. Obviously, I could not bring in a witness who would exaggerate, who would so overstate the case that the committee would not pay much attention to it. Eliminating that kind of witness, I still had problems. I could not use someone who would freeze in the presence of congressmen in the august hearing rooms of the Capitol—and that scene can be awfully impressive to a mill hand from Gastonia, North Carolina—but on the other hand, I also did not want a witness who would look on his or her appearance as a sort of stage debut and set out to dazzle the committee members.

To compound *these* problems, I obviously could not conduct this "talent hunt" myself. I had to rely on the various locals, explaining to them as carefully as I could, by letter or telephone, what I wanted.

There are three of these witnesses whom I recall most clearly, the first because Arthur Goldberg, then chief counsel for the CIO (he later was an associate justice of the Supreme Court and still later United States representative to the United Nations), won't ever let me forget. Arthur was involved in this particular hearing, and I had a "victim witness" whom I thought would make a most favorable impression. I had talked to her, and she had struck me as a levelheaded and intelligent woman. I had given her a general idea of the sort of questions that I thought she would be asked (since the spontaneity of her answers was what I wanted to impress the committee, it would have been stupid of me to try to coach her), but the only specific advice I gave her was to show up looking her best.

Goldberg and I were seated side by side at the counsel table in the committee room the next morning when my "victim witness" walked in.

She was wearing a mink stole.

At fifty cents an hour, a mink stole? I almost fainted.

It turned out that the members of her local, when they had heard of her forthcoming appearance before a congressional committee in Washington, had raised every nickel they could beg or borrow and had bought her the stole as a testimonial present.

I prefer to retreat into merciful silence on that one, though she handled it well enough by simply explaining exactly what had happened.

The second "victim witness" was a girl employed in the big Dan River Mills in Danville, Va. I remember her vividly because she told the committee an incident that illustrated most graphically what the poverty of textile wages meant to a mill worker.

She recalled that only a few years before, when she had been a youngster—about twelve or fifteen—she and her brother had found an injured dog lying alongside the railroad tracks. They had taken it home and nursed it back to health.

"But then we had to give him up," she told the committee.

"Why?"

And she answered, "I don't know if you gentlemen remember what it's like to be young and to want a dog and not be able to afford it. We had to give him up because we just plain didn't have the money to feed him."

Congressmen are not insensitive. They might have torn a professor of economics to shreds, but there was nothing more they wanted to ask this witness about textile wages.

The third of the "victim witnesses" was a young woman from Gastonia where there was a heavy concentration of spinning mills but where, nonetheless, few workers earned more than the minimum wage. In the course of her testimony, it was brought out that she was the sole support of a twelve-year-old daughter.

A Republican member of the House Labor Committee at this time was Ralph Gwinn from Bronxville, New York—elderly, impeccable, well spoken, and formidable. He prided himself on being able to take labor witnesses apart, always watching for the slightest hesitation or slip of the tongue.

My witness explained how the rent on her company-owned house and the bills for her electricity were always taken out of her paycheck in advance, along with her water bill (even though the water was supplied from a public tap a block from her home, where she had to walk to get it). There was, of course, no toilet in the house, she told the committee, so that everyone had to use a commode in the back yard. She had kept records on exactly what her rent, etc., had cost her, along with her food bills, clothing, doctors, dentists, and so on.

Nonetheless, she told the committee proudly, by literally watching every penny, she had been able to save a little.

It was at this juncture that Mr. Gwinn chose to intervene.

"Well, madam," he said, "we are glad to hear that you are doing so well. Pray tell us what you would do with the extra money if the minimum wage were increased?"

Without a moment's hesitation she answered, "I'd be able to afford to pay for piano lessons for my daughter. Everyone says she can play so well, and those I can't afford. Even in North Carolina, Mr. Congressman, we cannot live by bread alone."

There was a moment of dead silence. Then the chairman said, "The witness may be excused. She has made her point."

My technique must have worked. We got minimum wage increased to sixty-five cents an hour.

I have one final reminiscence of that period in my lobbying career. It has been my pleasure to hand at least a half-dozen senators in my career a one-thousand-dollar bill in a plain envelope. One was Estes Kefauver, and I will never forget the expression on his face when he saw it.

It was all perfectly legal. The money had been collected by

the union from its members by voluntary contributions for political funds and was duly reported to the Senate Campaign Committee.

But I had suggested that, instead of simply writing out a check and mailing it to the particular senator's campaign fund, we get the actual bill and that a representative of the union hand it over personally.

There's a little vanity in all of us. It's wonderful to see how the eyes of a US senator light up when he sees a one-thousand-dollar bill.

Chapter Twelve

ALTHOUGH I BELIEVE most profoundly that trade unions should be truly democratic institutions, and although in all of my workers' education courses I emphasized repeatedly my belief in the necessity for establishing a truly representative system for the election of union officers and for responsible attention to the loyal opposition, I must admit that democracy is the exception rather than the rule in the trade-union movement.

Lack of democracy, I am convinced, can threaten the future of trade unionism in this country; it can cut away at the base of its strength as a social force. One need only remember that after the years and years of work and negotiation that it took to bring the AFL and CIO into even the semblance of a common union, two of the biggest and most important unions—the Teamsters and the United Auto Workers (UAW)—are not now members of the AFL-CIO. That this is due in no small part to the commanding temperaments of three men—George Meany, James L. Hoffa, and Walter Reuther—I think emphasizes rather than detracts from my argument. If the trade-union movement were democratic in its structure, their personalities, however strong, would not have such long-lasting and important effects.

Out of my own personal experience, I can demonstrate the result that such a flaw can bring about in an individual union, in this case, the Textile Workers.

The split in the Textile Workers, viewed objectively, I think, was a most unnecessary, disgraceful, and inexcusable event. Viewed subjectively, it was one of the most painful episodes in my entire career.

At its base was that the Textile Workers, like any other union, had no adequate mechanism for giving effective recognition to the views of the opposition. Our own government has a whole vast, complicated mechanism for ensuring that the majority cannot—at least over a period of time—trample roughshod over the rights of the minorities, nor the minorities over the majorities. The trade-union movement in this respect is lacking.

Against this background, the personalities of the two men involved in the Textile Union split—Emil Rieve and George Baldanzi, the executive vice-president—were able to tear the union apart.

The most tragic aspect of the whole affair was that the union needed both men. Each one was extremely valuable.

I had been intimately associated with Rieve and in a certain measure responsible for his early success—helping him formulate his ideas into policy, speaking in his stead, issuing press releases on his behalf, and so on—but I also enjoyed a close and warm personal relationship with Baldanzi.

Baldanzi was a warm and outgoing man, an attractive individual, a very effective speaker. He was imaginative, his mind was quick, he was able to instill enthusiasm and loyalty in the rank and file. Rieve was withdrawn and introspective to a degree that made it impossible for him to have casual personal relationships. Meeting the head of some local union, his face would not break into a warm and easy smile. Unlike Baldanzi, he couldn't instantly make the man feel at ease or important. Rieve was the thinker, the planner; he couldn't be carried off on some tangent by the day's event as could Baldanzi. He was a deeper analyst of the union's problems, a better administrator, and far beyond Baldanzi in his superb abilities at collective-bargaining negotiations.

When the split occurred in the union, I had to admit to myself that Rieve was the more essential man, but at issue was that the union, as an entity, needed both men, and it had no mechanism by which to retain both.

What made the split inexcusable was that there was really no substantive difference between the two men, no ideological split, no matter of principle. Baldanzi wanted to effect some changes in the top structure of the union, changes with which Rieve agreed in principle. He would have made such alterations, perhaps in a slightly different way than Baldanzi, but they were in basic agreement as to goals. Rieve disagreed with Baldanzi, but only in method.

It was then that personal jealousy began to raise its ugly head, and for this I must blame both men. The jealousy was made clear—in my mind, at least—at the Textile Workers convention in New York City in 1948 when the ovation Baldanzi's speech received from the delegates was so much greater than Rieve's that the difference in the public magnetism of the two men was painfully obvious. I am sure that Rieve must have felt that he, an older man now but the guiding light of the union, was being pushed aside by a younger and more charming man.

The upshot was that at the national convention in Boston in 1950, Rieve opposed Baldanzi's bid for re-election as executive vice-president. (As with most unions, the Textile Workers' constitution requires that all major officers stand for election at every convention.) At that point the die was cast, and the next few years were ones that I would never willingly go through again.

Such an open clash in an organization reverberates and re-reverberates. The lines are drawn. You're for one side or the other, and there can be no compromise—the War of the Roses revisited. Charges and countercharges flew back and forth. Rieve charged that Baldanzi was trying to wreck the union for selfish political motives; Baldanzi accused Rieve of preparing to fire every official who opposed him.

The final explosion took place at the national convention of 1952 when Baldanzi ran against Rieve for president and lost. Baldanzi then led his followers, a total of about twenty thousand members, out of the Textile Workers and formed his own union, the United Textile Workers.

It was a totally wrong move. The new union that Baldanzi set up simply didn't have the organization to function independently. It didn't have enough members; it didn't have enough of anything.

The cost of the split can be measured in financial terms. I would estimate that the Textile Workers lost $3 million in dues and organizing efforts. The non-financial losses were more crucial and much less easy to measure. I don't know how many of our young officers we lost, the bright young men and women who grew embittered by the folly of this battle between the Titans and simply left. The split thrust the union itself, in terms of such programs as organizing drives, back several years.

To repeat: Such a breach would have been avoidable, had there been some machinery for resolving it.

This is true of all major unions today. They were all set up primarily as power structures, and power structures they remain. This is understandable if you view their history. Set up in times of stress, they were constantly attacked from all sides by external forces—by employers first, by the forces of the state, the courts, and the police—and they could ill afford internal struggle. The union *had* to be a power structure to survive external hostility, it had to speak with one voice, it could not allow itself to be wracked by dissension. It elected a leader—more correctly, the man who had forged the union out of the fires of trouble and rivalry emerged as the leader—and he was to remain.

This process is entirely understandable, but as we have moved into a new era of unionism, I think that the labor movement will be forced by outside pressures into drastic structural changes unless it makes them itself.

The UAW, for example, is probably the most democratic of the major unions. Nonetheless, the union, through the late thirties, was so torn by a series of bitter factional struggles, mainly inspired by the all-out drive that the communists waged to gain control, that the union came within a hairsbreadth of destroying itself, much as the Electrical Workers did.

Those battles left such scars on the union that, even up to the time of Walter Reuther's death, those leaders who disagreed with Walter were loath to take him on in an outright fight for fear of starting another feud. This was through no fault of his, for Reuther, after he won his savage war against the communists, was so sure of himself and so dedicated to democratic principles that he always gave the greatest consideration to honest opposition.

Yet the new era of unionism requires structural changes that should make unionism less dependent on the accident of a great leader like Reuther.

There are two factors that make it imperative for internal reform to begin. One is that trade unionism is now an accepted institution in American life. It may not be loved by employers, but it is at least tolerated, and the public has come to understand and accept the need for trade-union organization. Thus the external environment is no longer as threatening as it was when the labor movement was being born before the thirties.

The other factor is that a new generation of workers has entered the movement. They do not remember the old battles, the old struggles, the old sacrifices for survival. This may be sad to older men, but it is a fact of life. The new generation of workers does not feel the external hostility toward unions that in the past made internal solidarity more important than internal democracy. The new membership, which has also attained a higher level of education, is increasingly restive under a union machinery that has not adapted to the changes of a new era.

If the leaders of the trade-union movement have not yet awakened to the dissatisfactions of its new, younger, and better-educated membership, they have just not listened carefully enough. This is the labor movement's own generation gap.

The trade-union movement must build a new solidarity, with internal democracy as its base. The memory of older battles in the minds of older leaders won't hold the membership for long. A power machine, if it persists, will look more and more like an inflexible "establishment," or even like a racket. The new democracy must come, and it had better come from within. If it comes soon enough, the labor movement will then begin to be able to grapple with the new problems and the new issues of our society.

At the moment, there seem to be no meaningful forces at work to alter the monolithic structures of most trade unions. I had very great hopes for change at the time of the merger of the AFL and CIO, though the real reason that the CIO tolerated the merger simply offers another illustration of how important a role the drive of power played. Reuther's basic reason for agreeing to merge with the AFL was very simply that he thought—wrongly, I'm totally convinced—that David J. McDonald was about to take his United Steelworkers out of the CIO, a move which would have left Reuther with a very second-rate organization.

Reuther and McDonald had never gotten along well personally. Walter was more or less the ascetic, totally dedicated to his work, intellectually of the first rank, unimpressed by the trappings of office. After all, the president of the UAW driving around (as he generally did) in a two- or three-year-old modest sedan when all of the major auto companies were competing to get him to accept one of their finest luxury models, eating lunch at his desk (as he frequently did), was a far different man than Dave McDonald, who loved fancy automobiles and was very much at home having a three-drink lunch at a fancy restaurant with the president of some steel company.

The differences between the two men went deeper than

that. McDonald always thought that he—coming from the Steelworkers—should have inherited the mantle of the sainted Philip Murray, that he should have been Murray's successor as president of the CIO. I can think of few top labor men less suited for the job. When Reuther was elected president, McDonald set out to make his life as miserable as possible.

I viewed this battle from my vantage point as a legislative representative in Washington. My opposite number in the Steelworkers was Frank Hoffman, an ex-Notre Dame football star. From the moment of Reuther's election, Hoffman became a major obstructionist at the meetings of the CIO legislative conferences in Washington. Hoffman would accuse the rest of us of being fatuous idealists, impractical dreamers, sacrificing any chance of getting legislation passed because of dedication to Reuther's wild doctrinaire beliefs.

We had enough troubles at the moment without this. The passage of the Taft-Hartley Act had virtually ended organizing, and some unions were actually losing members.

Reuther was very much disturbed at McDonald's actions. On top of that, to repeat, he was worried that McDonald might quit the CIO. I was convinced that even if McDonald had tried to, the Steelworkers were so loyal to the memory of Murray that McDonald never could have carried it off. But Reuther feared the possibility, and he agreed to merge with the AFL.

He knew the hazards of such a merger as well as any man. There was absolutely no way of convincing the old-line AFL leaders that this was not simply a surrender on the part of the CIO. To them, the CIO had only rebelled against the AFL in 1936 like a willful child to go off on some wild adventure of its own; now it had seen the error of its ways and was returning to the fold. To them, the merger was not a marriage between two equal partners; it was the return of the prodigal to the parent.

Even Meany felt that way.

More than once I mentioned my misgivings about the merger to Reuther, and his answer was always the same.

"John, I know all this myself. But on the practical side,

I've committed myself too far to back out, and as far as the ultimate good of the trade-union movement in the United States is concerned, I'm absolutely convinced that we can't go on forever having two parallel trade unions operating on two such diametrically opposed philosophies."

The merger took place, of course, in 1955, and if you take the cosmic-destiny view of history, it was inevitable.

In practicality, it has not worked out anywhere near as well as it could have, nor as well as many of us had hoped. In view of my misgivings, I nonetheless felt that the great contribution that the merger could make to the American trade-union movement would be on the local level, that at least the second level of leadership would begin to work together so that the idealism and vitality of the old CIO would inspire the new organization to become a real social force in the country. It did not happen.

There was a bitter irony in this, for here we were at a stage that should have been one of American labor's transcendent moments, filled with exhilaration and jubilation—the merger of the two great unions, for which so many men had worked for so long—yet almost immediately the weaknesses of the merger began to overwhelm its strengths.

In the legislative field alone, notwithstanding Hoffman's tactics, before the merger Paul Sifton and Donald Montgomery of the UAW and I had an effective working relationship by which we agreed to pursue a general course on any given issue, then proceed.

When the merger went into effect, an entirely new legislative committee was established through which we were supposed to function. A full-fledged bureaucracy was imposed upon us. I knew the new head of the legislative committee quite well—Andrew J. Biemiller, whom I had helped introduce into the trade-union movement when he was a young socialist and college economics instructor back in Philadelphia. Andy's instincts were all correct, but the problem was that whenever we suggested any legislative program he had to consider all the old hidebound AFL unions whose own special interests might be affected.

One particular problem that I remember came up when the first bill was introduced into Congress to regulate billboards on federally funded interstate highways. It was my position, and that of my CIO colleagues, that we should throw our weight behind this bill. To have allowed the unregulated erection of billboards along interstate highways would have been nothing short of a national disgrace. But when we brought this suggestion forward at a meeting of the legislative committee, we found that Andy had to take into account the attitude of the AFL sign-painters union, which was vehemently opposed to any sort of regulation on billboards whatsoever.

The dispute was not resolved on the basis of wiser heads prevailing. It was resolved when the federal government threatened to cut off funds for the highways, and some important unions, like the steel workers and the construction trade workers, saw the possibility of the loss of thousands of jobs simply because the sign painters, with only a couple of hundred jobs at stake, wanted to hold up the whole federal highway system.

It was a small issue, but it illustrates how the dead hand of craft unionism still bound the new AFL-CIO. I can imagine —in fact, I've seen—the industrial unions involved in some pretty savage disputes. But at least they were over major issues, not over whether a thirteen-million-member labor organization should refuse to take a stand on what had become a major public issue just because it felt it must protect every last job it had.

When Walter Reuther finally took the Auto Workers out of the AFL-CIO in 1967, after months of soul-searching, it was because he had finally come to the point of despair with Meany. Now Meany is not the thick-skinned, small-brained dinosaur that his enemies in the labor movement like to paint him. He is neither stupid, lazy, nor corrupt. But he is a victim of his own thinking. Faced with the problems of the 1970s, he thinks in the way of the 1930s.

Any number of issues kept arising between him and Reuther.

To mention one, communism. Not only is Meany essentially conservative, and not only had he been frightened of the power he saw the communists achieving in some of the CIO unions in the thirties (Meany was not alone in this among American labor leaders), but he had his own particular gray eminence—Jay Lovestone, once a dedicated communist but, since the thirties, a fanatical anti-communist who carried on a crusade against his former comrades not only in the United States but also (joyfully backed by the Central Intelligence Agency) in many foreign countries. In other words, there was nothing within his power that Meany would not do, at home or abroad, to combat communism. Reuther, on the other hand, while certainly no friend of the communists, wholeheartedly supported the John F. Kennedy approach of "building bridges" to communist nations by cultural and trade exchange and, early in 1967, was able to get the State Department to approve the visit to this country of five high-ranking Russian "trade union leaders" over vehement Meany–Lovestone protests.

Another Meany–Reuther issue was discrimination. I know of no CIO union that tolerates discrimination—and again, to give Meany his due, he would not tolerate it in the AFL if he had an effective voice against it—but when Reuther was working with the Reverend Martin Luther King, Jr. in civil rights and anti-poverty programs, Meany could not or would not take an effective stand against the flagrantly discriminatory practices of some of his most important unions, the building and construction trades.

By all odds, the most important issue between Reuther and Meany was a basic one, the function of a union—any union. Walter was passionately convinced that, in today's world, unions had to assume far greater responsibilities: not simply to embark on great new organizing drives to embrace the masses of the unorganized, non-union workers in all sorts of peripheral industries—the details of Walter's plans for token-dues payments and flexible wage scales are extremely promising—

but also to become an active social force by taking a strong part in action programs in poor neighborhoods. Walter was an activist and a pragmatist. He advocated not only putting money into social-action programs but involving union members in them, setting up workshops and holding classes.

Meany could see none of this. He would agree with Walter that such involvement was necessary, even that his own building trades should be more socially minded, but nothing could change his hard-core conviction that the first duty of a union is to its own dues-paying members.

As a labor man, my major worry in respect to the above is the future of the American labor movement. I see only the most grudging acceptance of the fact that this nation is undergoing profound changes and that the old standards of measuring the worth of a labor union are now simply not good enough.

Chapter Thirteen

I KNOW OF no single piece of legislation in the entire history of the Congress of the United States that took so long to get passed, from the time of the first formal moves to launch it to the final signature of the bill by President Dwight D. Eisenhower, as that authorizing the US to join with Canada in building the St. Lawrence Seaway. Sen. George Aiken of Vermont, one of the staunchest supporters of the Seaway legislation for many long years, was so impressed by the length of time it took that he put together a history of the legislation in which he points out that the first formal proposals were made in 1895 and that it had been supported by every president of the United States starting with Theodore Roosevelt.

It was not until May of 1950 that President Eisenhower finally signed it.

A look at any relevant map will make instantly clear the inevitable logic of the Seaway. An ocean-going vessel heading up the St. Lawrence River has no problems as far as Quebec. Even as far back as the 1890s, fairly big ships could navigate upstream to Montreal. But from Montreal to Kingston, the Ontario port where the St. Lawrence flows out of Lake Ontario, the river was so shallow that it would not take ships with a draught more than fourteen feet.

Since the Great Lakes reach almost halfway across the continent, it did not take much imagination to realize that if the shallow stretch of the St. Lawrence between Montreal and Kingston—some 170 miles—were made navigable to ocean-going vessels, a vast area of North America would be opened to the cheapest form of commercial transportation. Beyond that, during the first third of this century it became equally apparent that the Seaway would be able to generate vast amounts of hydroelectric power, the cheapest source of electricity, for the Canadian provinces of Ontario and Quebec and, in the United States, for New England and New York.

So much for the inevitable logic of the proposal. Now for the inevitable logic against the proposal. Whose ox would be gored?

First, that of the railroads, particularly the American railroads serving the northeastern quarter of the country.

Second, that of the northeastern Atlantic seaports, particularly Boston and Philadelphia.

Third, that of the power industry primarily in New England, which was increasingly producing power by burning soft coal. This industry had huge investments in its existing plants and transmission systems, employed tens of thousands of workers, and represented the investment of hundreds of millions of dollars.

Fourth, that of the soft coal industry, which supplied the fossil fuels that enabled these plants to operate.

I list all these "anti" forces to re-emphasize my firm thesis that, to be realistic and effective in public lobbying, it is not enough to determine that you think such and such a piece of legislation is "good" or "bad." The effective lobbyist must immediately take the next step and recognize that what is "good" to him may be "bad" to the next man. The reason, I think, that many crusaders are so ineffectual in influencing legislation is that they never take this second step. They never understand that mere passionate conviction and impassioned pleading doesn't influence many congressional votes.

An incident that once happened on the Senate floor comes to mind. Sen. Robert Wagner had made a brilliant speech in support of the housing bill of which he was a co-sponsor, and, as he moved back toward his seat, Sen. Robert Taft of Ohio (not then yet convinced of the need for public housing, as he later became), leaned from his side of the aisle and held out his hand.

"Magnificent speech, Bob," Taft said. "Too bad you don't have the votes."

That is what the effective lobbyist must always keep in mind. The votes. That is what the St. Lawrence Seaway, for so many decades, did not have—the votes.

The problem was not simply the industrial forces that opposed us. It was also that these forces were in conflict among themselves. The Great Lakes ports—Buffalo, for example—were strong supporters of the Seaway as opposed to the Atlantic ports, and the water shipping interests were fighting the railroads.

Moreover, the labor unions themselves were in conflict, extramurally and intramurally. The Railroad Brotherhoods opposed the Seaway for obvious reasons—its collective members manned the trains that not only hauled bituminous coal to New England but also carried freight out of Boston, Philadelphia, and Baltimore. The Mine Workers were against the Seaway, though I must say, in all fairness, that neither the Railroad Brotherhoods nor the Mine Workers ever actively lobbied against it. Which was smart of them. They realized that in the long run it could damage their standing in the eyes of workers in general if they showed up working hand in glove with the power lobby and the coal interests.

But this congeries of conflicting interests could play the devil with a labor lobbyist in Washington working for the bill.

I remember once talking about the problem with Dan Flood—Rep. Daniel Flood of Wilkes-Barre, Pennsylvania, an urbane congressman known for his impeccable and dandified clothes, his waxed mustache, and the fact that he was an ex-actor of sufficient distinction to have played with Katherine Cornell in Theater Guild productions. No one could ask for a better liberal in the House than Dan—but he came from a coal-mining district.

"John," he told me, "you know me, and you know I'm for the Seaway one hundred percent. But you know my district. A 'wrong' vote on this, and what do I say to my constituents the next time I'm up?"

I think that I first became interested in the Seaway project entirely out of romanticism. It seemed like such a beautiful concept, so clear and logical, yet so patently doomed to failure. With few exceptions, the entire New England congressional delegation had opposed it for decades, and with that solid block of opposition, where were the votes coming from?

For a number of years, I must confess, I did nothing much except think about it. I had a great many other lobbying tasks, and there was no point in my lobbying against the interests of other unions, notably those of the Mine Workers.

When I first went to work as a lobbyist for the Textile Workers in Washington in 1943, it did not take me long to realize that when any textile company was authorized by the government, as a company engaged in the production of materials essential to the war effort, to construct a new plant, that plant was always in the South. That did not surprise me, for the textile industry for years had been slowly moving south because of cheap labor, but now I noticed that the industry was employing a new rationale in its arguments with the government for the location of new plants—the marked step-up in the insistence on the availability of cheap power.

I was not entirely a novice in the field of electrical power. When Franklin Roosevelt first came into office, one of the problems to which he had turned his attention was the dearth of electricity in rural communities and on farms, simply because the power companies found it unprofitable to run power lines into those areas. Roosevelt established the Rural Electrification Administration (REA) to fill this need, and it was overwhelmingly successful. The farmers and rural communities established cooperatives that both generated and distributed low-cost electricity with a relatively small capital expenditure advanced by the REA. Naturally, the private companies howled and launched a highly expensive campaign to prove that the REA was "socialistic" and that the money it advanced was paid by the taxpayers, which was not true. The money was advanced only in the form of interest-bearing loans that had to be repaid.

To counteract the power-company campaigns, the cooperatives formed the National Rural Electric Cooperative Association, headed by an ex-Arkansas congressman named Clyde Ellis, who gave up his political career to head the association. Ellis recognized that he needed a power base wider than one based on rural communities and farmers. He wanted the support of organized labor. He approached me, and in turn I approached Paul Sifton and Don Montgomery, about setting up a joint consumer-labor coalition to support rural electrification. Sifton and Montgomery were able to get the support (and financing) of Walter Reuther, and together we set up the Electric Consumers' Information Committee. Shortly afterward, the committee began to get support from the National Farmers' Union, from the Communications Workers of America, and from the national CIO itself.

My work with this information committee led me to believe that the Seaway could bring cheap power to the Northeast and undercut one of the principal arguments of mill owners for moving south.

My active lobbying for the Seaway had a curious quality to it. For one thing, I certainly enjoyed no mandate to do it. The Textile Workers were only "sort of" for the Seaway, for while the union agreed that the Seaway would benefit its locals in the Northeast, it still had visions of being able to do a real organizing job in the South; if it could, the problems of the Northeast from the strictly parochial view of the national union headquarters would not be so desperate. Additionally, I could expect no help from the national CIO offices, despite the financial support I had been able to wangle. Phil Murray was certainly not going to authorize the Textile Workers to lobby for a bill that already had the Mine Workers growling, and I knew better than to even mention it to him.

I had one advantage in my lobbying, however. Through Solomon Barkin, I had gotten to know Dr. N. R. Danielian ("Dan," everyone called him), who had headed the lobbying for the Seaway for years. Barkin and Danielian were both trained economists who had worked together in the early days of the New Deal. When Sidney Hillman put up the money to establish the Textile Workers Union, Barkin, a friend of Hillman's, went off to New York to become research director for the Textile Workers. Danielian stayed in Washington to lobby for the Seaway and eventually became director of the St. Lawrence Association, a citizen body formed in 1944 to promote the Seaway. I first got to know him well when his organization joined the National Electric Consumers' Information Service.

The great advantage of knowing Danielian was that whenever I needed data about the Seaway, I could obtain it from his office with no trouble at all. Danielian's association had much better resources than I, since it was being supported by all the states and most of the cities located on the United States side of the Great Lakes, plus innumerable banks and other financial institutions, and such corporations as the Ford Motor Company—all of which stood to gain from the Seaway. Danielian's role in the Seaway lobbying was without question by far the most important.

A number of developments combined to achieve final passage of the final Seaway bill. One was the signing of an agreement by President Harry S Truman and Prime Minister Louis St. Laurent in 1951 providing that if the US Congress didn't approve US participation "within a reasonable period of time," Canada would construct the Seaway on her own side of the river, and Canada and a private American company would jointly develop the power facilities. Another was that the American steel industry suddenly realized that the reserves of iron ore in the Mesabi Range in Minnesota were rapidly being depleted, that it would have to look to Labrador for future high-grade supplies. So this industry now switched in favor of the Seaway.

This particular development made a deep impression on President Eisenhower and his cabinet of multimillionaires. The president, who for months had been telling reporters that the issues involved in the Seaway bill were too complex and controversial to enable him to take a stand, now decided that he favored it. On the realistic political side, his belated approval carried more weight than the solid, long-time support of President Truman had.

There was also an unusual amount of political logrolling involved in the passage of the Seaway bill. When it was first introduced, there were also bills up for a study of the power possibilities of the tides in Passamaquoddy Bay between Canada and Maine—a perennial favorite since the days of Franklin Roosevelt—and for a development project on the upper Colorado River. It was made clear to all concerned with those bills that a vote against the Seaway would ensure a vote against them.

One of the key votes in the Senate was that of John Kennedy. The railroad lobby later said that it was I who had influenced Kennedy to vote for the bill, but that was not really so. I was aware of all the pressures that Kennedy was under, both as a senator from Massachusetts and, specifically, being closely associated with the port of Boston. The most lobbying I had ever done for the Seaway with Kennedy was to talk at length with him about how unprincipled I felt it would be for any senator not to vote for the development of such a great natural resource. There were many senators with whom I would never have bothered to use such an argument, but I had the feeling that it might work with Jack Kennedy because I also felt even then that his ambitions lay beyond the United States Senate.

At the end of my talk with Kennedy, which took about half an hour, he gave me no indication as to whether my little lecture had made an impression on him. But a month before the final vote was due to come up, I got a call from Kennedy's office asking if I could supply printed documentation for the shipping figures that I had cited to the senator.

I knew then how Jack was going to vote.

Danielian's office was able to obtain the information within a couple of hours, and I sent it over to Kennedy's office.

The day that Kennedy delivered a fifteen-minute speech on the floor of the Senate in favor of the Seaway, I said to myself, "He's going to run for president, and he's going to use that speech to get votes when he campaigns in the Great Lakes states."

He did, too.

When he was running for the presidency in 1960, the Textile Workers were holding their national convention in Chicago, and Jack was the principal speaker. After the session, he dropped by our convention offices with his sister Eunice, and I mentioned to him that in this part of the country his Seaway vote would certainly do him no harm.

He winked at me.

"John," he said solemnly, "do you think that I would cast a vote in the United States Senate just to get votes?"

I received a similar sort of backhanded compliment from Phil Murray. At the CIO convention at which the Seaway resolution was finally approved as part of the CIO legislative program, I had studiously avoided any connection with it because I knew how tricky a problem it was for Murray. I'm sure that he understood it, too, for as he was walking away from the platform at the end of the convention session, he passed near me, and with that canny Scotch look and that faint Scotch burr, he said, "I wouldn't see your fine finger in that Seaway resolution, would I?"

Chapter Fourteen

EARLY IN 1971, I was pleasantly surprised to find in my morning mail a booklet sent to me by my old friend and co-worker, William L. Batt, Jr., son of the late William L. Batt, formerly board chairman of S. K. F. Industries and one of the outstanding Republican businessmen brought into the New Deal by Franklin Roosevelt in the very early 1930s.

My Bill Batt had continued his father's tradition of public service and had been first administrator of the Area Re-Development Administration when it was established in 1965; the pamphlet he sent me was *Coalition Building for Depressed Areas—1955–1965*, by Roger H. Davidson, assistant professor of government at Dartmouth College. The official Labor Department definition of a "depressed area" is one in which "unemployment is now six percent or more of the labor force and where the average unemployment rate has been at least fifty percent above the national average for three of the last four calendar years. . . ."

I was delighted to receive the pamphlet because the Depressed Areas bill was the last one of my lobbying career in which I had taken a really significant part and because Professor Davidson had so emphasized the "coalition" approach to effective lobbying that I had been harping on for years.

It is my view that none of the liberal groups now active in the United States on behalf of social-reform measures can succeed in accomplishing their objectives unless and until they are able to build extensive and well-knit coalitions, each dedicated to a specific purpose but all functioning together vigorously, efficiently, and with unified direction.

My last quarter century of lobbying in Washington for labor proved to me over and over again, if nothing else, that organized labor, for example, standing alone, simply has not the political muscle to achieve its legislative ends. In fact, labor's mere size and single-minded purpose have sometimes created both hostility toward and jealousy of its programs that have resulted in defeats on major legislative issues where victories had seemed certain.

The success of the effort to enact legislation for the relief of depressed areas, extending in my own personal experience over fifty years, is an outstanding example of how a coalition can work.

By the end of the 1940s, economists and statisticians began to use the term "depressed areas," but they were nothing new on the American economic scene. The Mine Workers had known them for decades. In the Cumberland Valley, for example, the mining companies had traditionally simply closed up shop and moved somewhere else when a coal seam was exhausted. We in Textiles had known depressed areas for decades, particularly in New England.

At any rate, my work for the Area Re-Development Act as such began about 1950 when the Celanese Corporation closed its tire-cord plant in Cumberland, Maryland, for an indefinite number of months in order to install new machinery that could capitalize on recently discovered chemical processes for the manufacture of artificial cord for tires.

Cumberland is a cramped and drab factory city of about forty thousand people in far western Maryland (second largest city in the state), located in a setting of great natural beauty. It had been built along a series of valleys running down to the Potomac River overlooking a deep gorge called "the Narrows," which, besides being beautiful, is the gateway west. It is for that reason that the city was founded as the site for Fort Cumberland during the French and Indian wars, and that it later handled the freight (mostly bituminous coal) for four major railroads.

What made the shutdown of the Celanese plant important to us at Textiles was that, with twelve thousand employees, it was the largest single plant in the country to have a contract with us. (Wesley Cook, director of the synthetics division of the Textile Workers, had his office adjoining mine at our headquarters, and he was the first to tell me how bad the situation was; even after Celanese reopened, it planned on operating the plant with a work force of only six thousand, meaning that six thousand workers would be unemployed in a city of forty thousand.) But the shutdown had wider repercussions, as such shutdowns always do. The Chesapeake & Ohio, which handled much of the Celanese shipping, was forced to begin curtailing its operations in the city; a number of coal mines in adjoining West Virginia, which supplied Celanese with fuel for its power, began to shut down. The *Washington Post* ran a series of articles on the problems in Cumberland. (A classic book, *Night Comes to the Cumberlands,* by Harry M. Caudill, was published in 1962, though it concerned itself almost totally with the problems of the mine workers.)

At Textile headquarters, we decided that Sol Barkin would write a series of memoranda on the need for special legislation dealing with such special problems as existed in Cumberland. Sol and I jointly put out a series of bulletins on depressed areas, he doing the statistical and analytical work and I turning it into language that the average layman could understand. Sol is a topflight economist and a relentless taskmaster, especially on himself, but layman's prose is not his forte. The depressed area bulletins turned out to be unexpectedly successful—they attracted the attention of quite a number of congressional staff men and of a small group of newspaper correspondents.

Once Sol's basic memoranda had been written, we at Textiles set about organizing popular and congressional support to turn their ideas into legislation.

Our method of organizing popular support illustrates the point I wish to make about the necessity for coalitions working together.

First, as always, we had to establish a committee, which we euphemistically titled the Area Employment Expansion Committee because we learned very early that the term "depressd area" tended to alienate the very people whose support we wanted. You could see businessmen wince when the term was applied to their community; the Chamber of Commerce would send formal letters of protest, local newspapers would run editorials about it. We substituted the euphemism, and we ended by having more than a hundred Chambers of Commerce supporting us. The bill was finally passed as the Area Re-Development Act.

In Washington, we gained the support of the Rural Electric Consumers' Association and of the National Farmers Union, a staunchly liberal organization. We received the support of the representatives of the Indian tribes by amending our proposal to make Indian reservations eligible for assistance. And, of course, we got the support of other trade unions. I estimate that the AFL-CIO and its international unions spent some twenty thousand dollars lobbying for the Re-Development Act.

But, money aside, we now had as broad a coalition as we could manage for support of our program.

We needed a head for the committee, and Bill Batt found him—an ideal man, Prentiss Brown. (Bill at this moment was secretary of labor for the able young governor of Pennsylvania, George Leader, and Leader—much of whose state was on the verge of becoming an industrial disaster area—gave him authority to do as much work as he could for our committee.)

Prentiss Brown could not have been a better choice. In addition to his personal abilities and qualities, which were numerous, he was ideally suited to appeal to the business community—he was chairman of the board of the Detroit Edison Company. He was also ideally suited to appeal to the liberals. He was a former Democratic US senator from Michigan; and his home was in the "Upper Peninsula" of Michigan, a notoriously depressed area ever since the closing down of the lead mines there nearly a generation earlier.

One final person who played a key role on our committee was Charles S. Murphy, a genial and astute lawyer in Washington who had been brought up on a farm in North Carolina. Charley had worked in the Legislative Drafting Office of the US Senate and at this particular moment was in private practice in Washington. (He later became a White House aide to President Truman.) But we knew that, because of his personality, his work with the Senate, and because he was a hard-working Democrat, he would give us entrée to the Democratic National Committee and to the leadership of the Senate—specifically, to Lyndon B. Johnson, John F. Kennedy, Paul Douglas, and J. William Fulbright, all of them strong-willed to a man and as touchy with one another as so many strange cats.

With the committee set up and our support established, Barkin and I set about looking for congressional sponsors for our proposed legislation.

In the Senate, our man was Paul Douglas.

The Textile Workers had always had a strong bond with Douglas. A former professor of economics at the University of Chicago, he had enlisted in the marine corps in World War II, emerged with an almost-disabled arm, and in 1948 had decided to run for the Senate. We in Textiles were so impressed with him that we became his first trade-union backers; as a matter of fact, one of our best organizers in the area, Douglas Anderson, resigned from the union to become Douglas's first staff member.

I don't mean to suggest that Douglas sponsored the Re-Development Act because of any moral or emotional debt he might have felt he owed to the Textile Workers. He had an ice-cold mind, and he would have told us to go peddle our papers if he hadn't been convinced that our bill was a vital one.

On the House side, our strong man was Dan Flood of Wilkes-Barre, Pennsylvania. Douglas had depressed-area problems in Illinois, but Flood had worse ones. He too had a bond with the Textile Workers, though not so direct as that of Douglas. The textile industry had expanded considerably around the Wilkes-Barre area in World War II because it was not an area that could attract "glamour industries" like aircraft manufacturers; the textile manufacturers were thus able to find a ready supply of labor among the wives and daughters of the anthracite coal miners of the area. During the war, Textiles had built up a fairly good joint board in Wilkes-Barre; it frequently held educational meetings on Sunday mornings. Dan Flood, after attending mass on Sunday, would often drop in at these meetings. The ending of the war had sharply reduced the need for both textiles and anthracite coal, and Dan soon became one of our key sponsors on the Hill. When the Area Employment Expansion Committee held one of its working dinner meetings, as it did every few weeks at the Hotel Congressional, a great hangout for Hill people located just behind the old House Office Building, Flood was certain to show up.

The legislative struggle to pass the depressed areas bill began during the first Eisenhower administration.

Senator Douglas introduced his bill on July 28, 1955, and it was referred to the Senate Labor subcommittee.

Almost immediately, we began to run into problems. The first was major, and it concerned President Eisenhower's attitude toward the bill. Until he became president, I had never met Mr. Eisenhower, but I had hoped that he would be sensitive to the depressed-areas problems. Part of my difficulty in dealing with President Eisenhower was that he seemed to be barricaded behind a staff jealous of protecting him to the extent that it, itself, seemed afraid to discuss public problems. I was not a novice at dealing with White House staff members, and in previous administrations I had not hesitated to discuss my position with them. They knew that I was a partisan pleader, they knew I certainly was not stupid enough to think that I could—had I even wanted to—find out anything about the inner workings of the president's office, but these earlier aides were perfectly capable of saying, "Well, now, John, that's your side of the story. But on the other hand, you have to remember . . ." and so on. Eisenhower's staff members seemed to be afraid of telling you what time it was. In addition, it was hard to determine Mr. Eisenhower's attitude on any issue.

I grew somewhat optimistic when, shortly after Paul Douglas introduced his bill, Mr. Eisenhower asked the Congress to adopt what he called "a domestic Point Four Program." The optimism vanished when his administration bill, introduced by Sen. Alexander Smith, arrived on the Hill. The bill proposed a funding of $50 million, compared to the $390 million in the Douglas bill, and most experts had said that the Douglas figure was too low.

The next problem was the sort of intrapolitical one in the Senate that you have to learn to live with as a lobbyist. It involved the four men I have already listed: Johnson, Kennedy, Fulbright, and Douglas. The off-year elections of 1954 had made Johnson majority leader in the Senate, a position of enormous power and influence. Johnson, in the narrower sense of politics, was the greatest politician I have ever known. (In the broader sense, it was Franklin Roosevelt.) Johnson had an instinctive knowledge, it seemed—I'm sure it was part instinct and part long experience—of what could and what could not be done on Capitol Hill. He had an almost eerie sense of judgment about his fellow senators and how they would react—he knew when to reason, when to cajole, when to menace; he knew which argument would appeal to one senator and not to another; he knew all their strengths and weaknesses. He could be enormously charming when he chose; he could be intimate and confiding; he could be blunt and coarse; he could be folksy; he could become a raging savage. And with all that, I always felt that whether he was laughing or ranting or folksy, there was always something behind it—some power, some strength that he was directing to what he was doing so that you were never seeing the real man.

Senator Douglas was always somewhat of a loner on the Hill, well respected but not a close, intimate man. Even after seven years on the Hill (at this time), his fellows were still inclined to think of him as "the professor" rather than as a politician. He could be as charming as Johnson, though in a different way, in private or with a few other people, but away from informal occasions he always seemed aloof and reserved. His charm, I always felt, went deep into his being and came from an inner warmth, whereas with Johnson I always thought he was *deliberately* being charming; that, as with an actor, it suited his purposes of the moment.

As for Fulbright, I always considered him basically much more conservative, certainly on domestic issues, than most other people thought him. I also had the feeling—and I must confess that it was no more than that—that he was somewhat disappointed, deep inside, that the Democratic party had never nominated him for the vice-presidency. (I'm sure he was far too realistic, except in daydreams, to think that he would ever have a chance at the presidency.) It didn't take a very astute political observer to guess that Fulbright would be against the Area Re-Development Bill.

Jack Kennedy was already a rising star on the Hill, and, strangely enough, he had many characteristics similar to Johnson's. It is odd how much alike they were in their differences. I always thought that Jack's charm was more genuine than Johnson's, that he was capable of warm, close relationships. (I mean politically, not in the personal sense, where they both were.) Jack's anger was likely to be ice cold, whereas Johnson's would explode. Of course, Jack had nowhere near Johnson's experience either in politics or on the Hill, but he too seemed to have that politician's instinct for how people would act or react, what to say to this man and not to that.

But, above all, they were both strong-minded, strong-willed, single of purpose. I think that each, perhaps only unconsciously, recognized the other as cut from the same piece of cloth; each saw in the other the enemy. Johnson was the old tiger, veteran of a thousand political battles, still at the height of his powers but aware that, where he had once been the challenger, now there were younger tigers emerging to challenge him. Jack Kennedy was one of the younger tigers.

The first legislative difficulty involved the differences among these four men. Immediately after the bill was introduced, it was referred to the Senate Labor subcommittee, of which Jack Kennedy was chairman. Fulbright, of the Banking and Currency Committee, decided that one of *his* subcommittees should handle it. Why he did this, I shall never know. I didn't feel that he was strongly enough against the bill to want to kill it in committee. I can only guess that he wanted to override Kennedy.

Fulbright got his way—he had considerably more seniority and power in the Senate than Jack Kennedy—but we of the Area Expansion Committee knew that we were in trouble and immediately set to work. A favorable report from Fulbright's committee was a touch-and-go situation. I was on the phone almost constantly trying to enlist people of any possible influence with members of the subcommittee to use their weight to get the vote; Charley Butler was trying to persuade Lyndon Johnson to let it be known that he was for the bill; Douglas was using his strength to get votes as, of course, was Kennedy.

Because of his reasoned, almost academic, approach to social and economic problems, Douglas had almost as much influence with Republicans on the Hill as he did with Democrats, and he came up with a major coup. He approached old Fred Payne—Frederick G.—the crusty and hardheaded Republican senator from Maine, and proposed a joint approach to the bill. (Payne had his share of depressed areas in his state.) If Payne would support the bill, Douglas would have it proposed under joint Douglas–Payne sponsorship.

Payne agreed, and it was his support that finally got the bill out of committee. Douglas was not alone in working on Payne, of course. It is extremely rare for one senator-to-senator agreement to swing a vote in the upper house. There are far too many political considerations on both sides; both senators have to see an advantage in the vote. We at Textiles—in good part because there was a very effective AFL-CIO council in Maine—were able to add our arguments and the strength of our position to Douglas's.

With Payne's help, the bill came to a vote on the Senate floor on May 13, 1958. It passed, 46–36.

We had naturally also been having our problems in the House. The bill had been assigned to Banking and Currency, had been reported out favorably, had been passed on the floor, and then had been referred back to the House Rules Committee, headed by my long-time enemy, Howard W. Smith of Virginia. Smith was an archetype of the popular image of the old-time Southern congressman. He was a very rich banker (this is not tautology) and farm owner. For years he habitually wore wingtip collars and in 1938 was one of the House members whom Franklin Roosevelt wanted "purged." As a theoretician, I don't approve of the executive branch infringing on the legislative branch, but in this case I'm only sorry that it didn't work. If there were any piece of legislation in the House that could even remotely be described as "liberal," Howard Smith would oppose it.

When the Area Re-Development bill went back to the Rules Committee, Smith promptly proceeded to bottle it up. To get it back out would require at least two Republican votes, and Dan Flood finally was able to persuade two Republican committee members to appeal to the White House for guidance on their votes. The president, as always, turned the appeal over to one of his staff, in this case Sinclair Weeks, a bumbling ex-senator from Massachusetts whom the president had had the misfortune to name secretary of commerce. Weeks, a millionaire, advised the president against support of the bill, which ended the bill for that session of Congress.

In the next session, Mr. Eisenhower more effectively demonstrated his lack of understanding of the complexity of the economic problems in which the nation was involved. When the Re-Development bill was passed by substantial margins in both Houses (46–36 in the Senate, 176–130 in the House), he pocket vetoed it.

After that, all of us involved in the problem felt that we

would simply have to wait for a new president who would understand more of the problems of the country than did Mr. Eisenhower.

When John F. Kennedy took his oath of office in January of 1961, we backers of the Re-Development bill were ready for action. As early as January 5, 1961, Senator Douglas met with forty-three congressmen who had agreed to be cosponsors of a new bill he proposed to introduce. (Between the November elections of 1960 and the beginning of 1961, Douglas had headed a task force on the problems of unemployment appointed by president-elect Kennedy.)

Douglas's new bill passed the Senate on March 15 by a vote of 63–27; the House bill passed March 29 by a vote of 251–167, and on May 1, "with great pleasure," President Kennedy signed the bill into law.

William Batt, Jr., was appointed administrator of the agency. The offices were installed in the Department of Commerce building on 14th Street in the space left vacant when the US Patent Office moved into its new buildings across the Potomac near the National Airport.

I can't analyze my feelings when I entered the Area Re-Development offices for the first time and suddenly remembered that these buildings had been put up during the administration of President Calvin Coolidge, when Herbert Hoover had been secretary of commerce.

And I also remembered walking these same corridors back in the 1930s, in the days of the New Deal, when the offices of the NRA were in the selfsame spot.

Chapter Fifteen

As I SAID, the Area Re-Development bill was the last piece of legislation that I really worked on as a professional lobbyist. Before I finally officially retired from my career in lobbying, I almost enjoyed an honor of which I would have been proud, had I received it. In 1953, shortly after President Eisenhower took office, the CIO submitted my name to the White House for assistant secretary of labor. The AFL and the CIO had not yet merged (the merger was in 1955), and the understood agreement was that if the president picked an AFL man as secretary of labor, the assistant was to be from the CIO. Mr. Eisenhower had chosen Martin Durkin, of the AFL, as his labor secretary. (The irreverent line about the makeup of the president's cabinet was "eight millionaires and a plumber.") Walter Reuther then named me his designate for assistant secretary.

I promptly ran afoul of Sherman Adams, Mr. Eisenhower's executive assistant. Although Adams came from New Hampshire, my snobbish New England friends kept telling me that he "wasn't a real Adams"—meaning that he couldn't trace his lineage directly back to Samuel or John Quincy. Adams greatly enjoyed the newspapers' description of him as a "flinty New Englander." He had been governor of New Hampshire; he had also been a floor manager at the convention that nominated Eisenhower and had been his first campaign manager. (The famous "vicuna coat scandal" involving Adams did not erupt until much later.) Adams was a very narrow and doctrinaire man.

When my name was submitted for nomination, the first thing Adams wanted was the file from the Federal Bureau of Investigation on me—and it was a thick one (including the fact that my father had been an anarchist and that I had been brought up in a socialist commune). Adams read the file and called Reuther. He asked, "What kind of guy is this you're sending me?"

Walter protested that he'd known me practically since the year one, that my record would show that I was a loyal American and a fighter against communism in the labor movement, but none of this would avail. Adams wanted my name withdrawn. Walter wrote him a four-page single-spaced letter listing the reasons he wouldn't. Adams still insisted.

Walter finally convened a meeting of the executive board of the CIO to explain what was going on. The board voted unanimously not to withdraw my name, and Walter wrote Adams a letter explaining his action. He told Adams that in view of the administration's stand, the CIO would submit no other name, and so the post remained unfilled.

In one way, I was relieved. I have always felt that the Labor Department is about as ineffective, uninspired, and inadequate a federal agency as exists, and I didn't really look forward to the duties of assistant secretary. On the other hand, it would, of course, have been an honor. I thought of Abraham Lincoln's famous story about the man who was tarred, feathered, and ridden out of town. Someone asked him how he felt about it. "Well," as Lincoln told the story, the man said, "if it hadn't been for the honor, I'd just as soon have walked."

I did get a good deal of publicity out of it, especially in the

London newspapers, which made much of my socialist connections there and the fact that I had worked as a newspaperman in London in my young days.

Toward the end of my career with the Textile Workers, a man named John Colao called at my office to discover if I would be willing to help with an organization then being built, the National Council of Senior Citizens. John had been an actor-singer (he had been on tour as one of the leads in "Der Rosenkavalier"), but during the Depression he had gone to work in an auto-parts plant in northern New Jersey and become a member of the staff of the UAW. When John Kennedy was running for president, Colao built an organization (his salary being paid by the UAW) among older men and women to help Kennedy's campaign.

I agreed to Colao's suggestion, without really giving it too much thought, for two reasons. One was that, in the course of my union duties and my inexorably mounting years, I had become increasingly interested in the problems of older workers, particularly in how their pensions and Social Security payments were increasingly being devoured by rising medical costs. (Ten years earlier I had been a member of the Committee on the Nation's Health, headed by Dr. Michael Davis, a renowned social worker who was also an authority on medical costs and related problems. This committee's espousal of the Murray-Wagner-Dingell bill, the first national health insurance bill, gave President Truman the necessary political leverage to get the bill passed, even though the relentless campaigning of the American Medical Association (AMA) forced the committee out of business within a couple of years.) The second was that a member of the House for whom I had great respect and affection, Aimé Forand of Rhode Island, was working hard on the problems of the aging and was himself sponsoring the Council of Senior Citizens.

The original motive that led to the formation of the National Council of Senior Citizens was political: to create an effective organization to press for the enactment of the Medicare bill. Long before this goal was reached, however, it became clear that the council was serving an even more important purpose in opening channels for the seniors themselves to contribute to community welfare and, through their own activities, to gain a fresh sense of their worth.

Many of the seniors' clubs that had previously been set up by churches and public-recreation departments were based on the desire of the sponsors to brighten the lives of elders by providing companionship and entertainment, arts and pastimes to while away empty hours. The council, on the other hand, gave them something to do, showed them work that needed to be done for others, not themselves. By participating, many for the first time, in the legislative process, they gained a sense of dignity, of recognition of their place and power as citizens. Many of them also developed an unsuspected capacity for leadership. Some became club leaders, blooming in their acceptance as leaders and basking in the recognition of their responsibilities. Many were appointed to local, county, and state committees formed to deal with the problems of older persons. Some became regular contributors to newspapers of opinions and problems of the elderly.

Among other discoveries made by our program was that an astonishingly large numer of elders had more or less dropped out of society. Many did not even know that they were entitled to Social Security benefits, let alone Medicare. Therefore, we established a program called FIND: for the Friendless, Isolated, Needy, and Dependent.

We established programs to encourage the employment of older persons, engaging them to work twenty hours a week at the prevailing minimum wages.

Other programs have since been devised by local community-action agencies, including the National Council of Senior Citizens. One is the "foster grandparents" program in which seniors spend five afternoons a week acting as grandparents to troubled children in institutions.

One of the first things that I did with the Senior Citizens was to help set up meetings around the country to try to form one solid organization with some kind of political clout. There were all kinds of groups of older people scattered around the country at that time, but they had no political power. A number of these groups, especially in California, dated back to the days of the Townsend Plan, founded in California in 1933 by Dr. Francis E. Townsend. Although it was fashionable to laugh at it, behind the Townsend Plan lay a certain amount of common sense. Dr. Townsend proposed that the federal government pay every citizen in the country over the age of sixty a flat two hundred dollars a month, with the proviso that the two hundred dollars be spent within the month and within the United States. You could not go off to Mexico and collect your payments while living on twenty dollars a month, fish and beans. Dr. Townsend proposed to finance the program by imposing a two percent federal sales tax. Actually, even today, the Social Security system does not pay two hundred dollars a month to everyone over sixty, and what it does pay for is funded through taxes, though not sales taxes. Perhaps Dr. Townsend was ahead of his time.

In any event, it was interesting, once I started helping forge the Senior Citizens, to suddenly get letters from grumpy old codgers around the country accusing me of trying to move in on Dr. Townsend's movement and asking me to attend their meetings and see how an organization for the aging should *really* be conducted. Since I had been under the impression that the Townsend Movement had more or less died a natural death in the 1930s, these letters came as a surprise in the 1960s, but I was delighted to get them.

Beyond attempting to make an effective organization for Senior Citizens, my reason for setting up the country-wide meetings was to attempt to fight the AMA's continuing, determined, well organized, and soundly financed campaign against any sort of Medicare program.

At the time I joined Senior Citizens, their meetings had drawn little attention, largely because neither the politicians nor the press had yet realized how many senior citizens existed, or how solid a bloc they formed. But when we began to get overflow crowds at meetings in such places as Houston, Cleveland, Providence (in the biggest auditorium in the state), Buffalo, Cincinnati, Indianapolis, and New York City (in Madison Square Garden), people began to pay attention to us.

At the Senior Citizens convention in Washington in the early spring of 1963, I allowed myself to be made secretary-treasurer of the council. (I say allowed myself because I knew the council didn't have much funds to be treasurer of. Our annual dues were one dollar.)

It was only a couple of months after President Kennedy's assassination that I found myself the president of the Senior Citizens Council. I had been working closely with Aimé Forand, then the president, and because he was several years younger than I, I had never given a thought to the state of his health until he called me at home one evening and said, "John, you're it."

Aimé had been at an Embassy reception during the evening and had suddenly fallen down. The doctors said that he had suffered a minor stroke and that he was to cancel all activity.

Actually, since by this time I was formally retiring from Textiles, I was glad to have a job—even though it paid no salary, and it took me some time just to get my expenses covered—without all the quarreling and politicking that normally went with running the presidency of anything. In addition, I was pleased, after all the years that I had spent as a staff member, to have some authority, to be able to speak in the name of the council, and to be able to direct the way in which I thought things should be run.

By far the biggest and most successful meeting we promoted for the Senior Citizens was that held on the afternoon of August 26, 1964, at the Democratic National Convention at Atlantic City (the convention that nominated Lyndon Johnson and Hubert Humphrey). John Bailey, the Democratic national chairman, was, I think, becoming more aware of the political power of the Senior Citizens, and he knew that our main objective, Medicare, coincided with one of the planks in the Democratic platform. Bailey agreed to turn over the convention hall to us for a couple of hours on the afternoon of August 26, to stage what we called the National Senior Citizens' Forum.

The size of the turnout of oldsters staggered even me, and

it positively stunned the delegates to the convention. One factor that I hadn't appreciated enough in advance was that, apart from the program planned, just the prospect of having an outing away from the prosaic life of a retiree, would bring the oldsters out in droves. We had sent invitations to seniors mainly around New Jersey, of course, but also in the neighboring states of New York, Connecticut, Pennsylvania, Delaware, and Maryland. The response was so enthusiastic that on the morning of the meeting we realized that we had better alert not only the Atlantic City police but the New Jersey state police as well. Even so, a monster traffic jam developed.

Besides all the private automobiles that showed up (thousands, I would guess, though we had no way of counting), there were 150 buses. We had not made a real effort to round up all the delegates to the Democratic National Convention for our session, except for about a hundred key men I wanted there, but when word began to circulate about the size of the meeting, the delegates began to show up in droves. A politician, better than enyone else, knows how hard it is to get people out for any meeting, especially one with the jazzy title of the National Senior Citizens' Forum. Politicians who had rejected our invitation to attend pushed their way up to the platform just to be introduced. There was no room left for me. I stood at the door of the vast convention hall and helped direct the seating, marveling at the spectacle.

For a program that we were forced to organize on fairly short notice, we fared none too badly. We had hired a local band and had put together a makeshift volunteer variety show from a number of professional acts that were then appearing in Atlantic City. For speakers, we had two distinguished sisters, Mrs. Margaret Schweinhaut, a state senator from Maryland who was also chairman of the state's commission on the aging, and Mrs. Marie McGuire of the FHA; and finally the main speaker, Rep. Carl Albert, the House democratic leader.

The success of the meeting had far-reaching effects. Not only did it get us a great deal of newspaper publicity—almost all the newsmen who were covering the convention for the newspapers and magazines, radio and television, carried the story of the meeting—but a good many of the delegates and candidates who had previously been inclined to write off Senior Citizens as a kind of ineffectual group of old dodderers suddenly realized that perhaps they had better take a second look. Our slogan, "Health Care for the Aging through Social Security," suddenly seemed to hold a lot more political bite than these politicians had originally thought possible.

Getting Medicare through the Congress in the short space of only about three years was due to a combination of circumstances, the first of which was the assassination of President Kennedy. A great many first-rate political scientists have already pointed out that President Johnson was a far more effective operator with the Congress than John Kennedy ever had been. But there is an added factor that I think the political scientists are inclined to minimize: Had it not been for the dreadful drama of Kennedy's death, Johnson would not have been able to move forward as he did. When I got to the Hill after the Kennedy funeral, I found most of the members in a mood of abnegation, filled with feelings of guilt about what they had not done. If Kennedy had been disgraced in some sordid sex scandal, they would cheerfully have impeached him; if he had died a natural death, they would have mourned him; but to have him shamefully assassinated produced in them thoughts of what might have been. If Johnson had asked Congress then to vote the money to buy Mars, I think they would have done so to a man—and woman.

The result was that President Johnson, filling out the final year of Kennedy's term of office, was able to push more liberal and progressive legislation through Congress than I think Kennedy would have been able to do even if he had served another full term. (I think that President Johnson may yet still be judged one of America's most effective presidents.)

Be that as it may, Johnson's success in his own first full term was also due to his resounding majority over Goldwater that carried into office enough liberally minded Democratic congressmen to enable us to get a solid number of progressive bills passed, including Medicare.

I did almost no direct campaigning in the 1964 elections, nor in 1966, but I worked intensively preparing materials for the congressmen who were campaigning on a Medicare platform, and I was very pleased that in both elections, especially in the 1966 off year, almost all the congressmen who campaigned on a Medicare platform were elected.

There was another factor, as in the great turnout at the Democratic National Convention, that I had initially overlooked in my work with Senior Citizens. That was that the seniors *like* to write letters. I mentioned much earlier how little attention the average congressman pays to the average petition and how quick he and his staff are to spot the "form" letter that is dictated by some organization. On the other hand, from the lobbying point of view, it is almost impossible to get the average trade-union member, or citizen, to sit down and write a personal letter, one of the most effective ways of influencing a congressman that I know of.

But the seniors would, and did.

By this time the Senior Citizens organization was taking on the semblance of a going concern. Many of the small groups that had existed before—Golden Years clubs, for example—joined us. We had branches in almost every state in the union. Though I had suffered a minor heart attack, and the doctors had told me to cut down on my traveling, I was still averaging about fifteen thousand miles a year visiting our locals. (I was preparing to step down as president of the Seniors, to be succeeded by Nelson Cruikshank, former research director of the CIO.)

We began publishing a newsletter for the local clubs, keeping them informed as to what was going on in Washington that affected their interests, and a good number of newspapers throughout the country—especially in New England, the Midwest, Florida, and California—began to realize that older citizens were forming an increasingly important part of their population. They began to run weekly columns on the doings of senior citizens.

The seniors themselves began to realize that the whole political process had a direct personal bearing on their lives, especially on the Medicare issue where doctor and drug bills were rapidly becoming so dominant an economic factor in their lives, overshadowing all other items in the cost-of-living standards.

During the last year or so of the Medicare struggle, the president's legislative lobbying staff met regularly at the White House, and I belive that I attended every one of those meetings.

In all my years of lobbying, I had been in the middle of a number of very intensive and well-organized drives to "get the votes" in Congress, but few of them involved as much head cracking as went on in the campaign for Medicare. The propaganda of the AMA about "socialized medicine" and "the entering wedge of socialism" was so subtle, pervasive, and well financed that old-time congressmen I normally could count on wouldn't even give me a commitment on their vote one way or the other, even privately.

We did eventually get the votes, however, under the leadership of Sen. Patrick MacNamara of Michigan and Rep. John Fogarty of Rhode Island, and when the bill finally passed the Senate-House conference, President Johnson decided that rather than have the official signing of the bill in the White House, as was customary, the signing would be held at Independence, Missouri, in the presence of former President Harry S Truman. Mr. Truman was in failing health at that time, though still bright and chipper when I saw him for the final time, and after all, Mr. Johnson felt, Mr. Truman had signed the first health-insurance bill, the Murray-Wagner-Dingell Bill.

On July 30, 1965, two air force jets flew from Bolling Field, just outside Washington, to Kansas City, Missouri for the official signing. The president flew in the first plane with the official government party and the White House correspondents, and Mrs. Johnson flew in the second plane with us commoners who had been invited to the ceremony.

It was a most satisfactory ending to my lobbying career.

Epilogue

JOHN W. EDELMAN died December 27, 1971 at his home in Arlington, Virginia, full of years and not uncrowned with honors, as he might have been forced to admit. He was a modest man who was fond of quotations from lesser-known British poets.

He had, in truth, many honors; of these the ones he treasured most were his invitation by President Johnson to fly with him to Missouri to be present at the signing of the Medicare Bill in the presence of former President Truman; the Arthur Reardon Award of the Washington Newspaper Guild (John was always an old newspaperman); a senatorial citation for his contribution to the St. Lawrence Seaway Bill; the request by Wayne State University for his personal files for its history of labor archives and that of Columbia University to participate in its program of "Living History."

Perhaps the one closest to his sentimental heart was the testimonial dinner given him at the old Willard Hotel in Washington in May of 1959, when he was in the process of retiring from the Textile Workers to take on the presidency of the National Council of Senior Citizens. Three of John's closest and oldest friends were responsible for organizing the dinner: Esther Peterson and Hyman Bookbinder, both from the old Amalgamated days, and Paul Sifton of the Auto Workers.

It was a remarkable dinner for the number of congressmen —who normally think of "lobbyist" as an eight-letter word— who came to pay tribute to John's years of public service. They, too, were old friends from the Hill; to name only the oldest (in terms of friendship) among almost a hundred: Senators Paul Douglas, Hubert Humphrey and James Murray; Representatives Richard Bolling, Carl Elliott, Daniel J. Flood, John Fogarty and George Rhodes.

If it is infeasible to list the members of Congress at the dinner, it is impossible—without an appendix—to list the others beyond a few: Andrew J. Biemiller, legislative director of the AFL-CIO; James B. Carey, president of the IUE; Edith Christenson of the Consumers Co-operative League; N. R. Danielian; Judge Henry Ellenbogen; Gardner Jackson; Leland Olds; Joseph L. Rauh, Jr.; Victor Reuther; Oskar Stonorov, and Mary Heaton Vorse.

The last two years of John's life, until almost the very end, were devoted principally to working on this book.

His memorial service was held, fittingly enough, in one of the hearing rooms in the Senate Office Building where he himself had so often testified.

It was Senator Frank Church who used a phrase that might aptly sum up John's life work: "He was a lobbyist—a lobbyist for all the people."

JOSEPH CARTER

Index